British Sporting *Greats*

British Sporting *Greats*

Introduction by John Inverdale

Edited by Annabel Merullo and Neil Wenborn

Contents

Introduction
John Inverdale

How many conversations have you overheard that included the line 'he was a great player, he was', only to find that the subject matter's sole claim to sporting sainthood was a crucial goal in a never-to-be-forgotten second round FA Cup tie in 1982? Everyone these days is a great player, great batsman, great jockey, great whatever. It's the revaluation – devaluation – of the language. In the same way that any record which scrambled into the Top Ten several decades ago is now a 'classic', so those who were once 'handy' on the sporting fields of Britain are now elevated to greatness. Occasions that were once memorable have become 'historic'.

And yet, amid the hyperbole, there are people, places and moments that can still genuinely be described as 'great'. Which is where this book comes in. You may be one of those who knows, as the cliché has it, exactly what you were doing when news came of Kennedy's assassination. For myself, I remember shaving while listening to the six o' clock news on 8 December 1980 and taking a huge chunk out of my face with the razor when I heard that John Lennon had been shot. Read Stephen Bayley's piece about James Hunt here and you share a moment in the history of sport that left a similar lasting mark on someone's life.

Then there's Hunter Davies writing about 1966 and all that, and Angela Rippon on the night 24 million people sat and watched ice-skating and listened to Ravel with Torvill and Dean. There are people and places that changed the direction of an individual's career, and with it our national sporting life: Sir Bobby Charlton on the man whose example, more than anything else, was responsible for attracting him into professional football, the great Sir Stanley Matthews; Virginia Wade on her lifelong fascination with 'the most valuable rectangle of grass in the world', the Centre Court at Wimbledon, where she was to join her tennis heroes and heroines in victory in the Queen's silver jubilee year. Here too are some of the great institutions of British sport, both in the abstract and in the life: Dickie Bird on the cricket umpire; Ian Botham on the Ryder Cup; Sir Henry Cooper on the Queensberry Rules.

And there is Reg Gutteridge describing an evening in 1963 which certainly made me realise that sport could excite like almost nothing else.

On the night that ''Enry's 'Ammer' decked Cassius Clay, a six-year-old boy lay in bed somewhere in the West Country, his transistor radio clasped to his ear, hearing those famous words from commentator Simon Smith: 'And Clay is down. Clay is down.'

I rushed out of bed.

'What are you still doing up?'

'Henry Cooper's knocked Cassius Clay out! Come and listen!'

He hadn't of course. In the time it took me to get from the bedroom to the sitting room and back to the bedroom, Clay, by fair means or foul – read Reg Gutteridge's view from the ringside – had bought a bit of time and Cooper's eye was badly cut. My eyes, though, had been opened for good.

Sporting highs and lows can provide a kind of soundtrack to our lives. Sitting transfixed in a school common room as England threw away a two-goal lead against Germany in 1970. Standing in a street outside a Radio Rentals shop watching Botham transform the Headingley Test. Staying up into the early hours of the morning in a B & B in the Yorkshire Dales to watch Coe against Ovett in Los Angeles. Slamming the phone down on my sister when she rang me during the penultimate frame of Dennis Taylor's world snooker final in 1985. 'Don't you understand?...'

And then in later years being lucky enough to witness at first hand some of those great sporting moments – moments which, as Duncan Goodhew says in his essay on Matthew Webb's first cross-Channel swim, somehow give us a sense of collective greatness, moments we can feel part of simply by witnessing them. Desert Orchid coming storming up the Cheltenham hill. Steve Redgrave's second, third and fourth Gold Medals (I missed the fifth because I was asleep!). Standing by the seventeenth at the Ryder Cup in Brookline as Justin Leonard's putt trickled inexorably towards the hole. Gazza and Becks. A succession of British winners of the Open championship. The constant striving of Tim Henman to win Wimbledon and break the biggest hoodoo in British sport.

And in the same way that you might associate Glenn Miller, the Stones, the Rollers or Madonna with your first marriage/divorce/car crash/job (delete as applicable), so, as Nick Hornby spelt out so clearly in his novel *Fever Pitch*, sport can do that too. Schooldays, or becoming a parent, can mean the furore of Greavesey not being picked by Sir Alf, or Lineker being substituted by Graham Taylor.

This book will probably include some of those sport-defining moments in your life, just as it does some of mine, but it couldn't possibly encompass them all. Let's face it: we're talking people and places, winners and losers, across seven decades and more. If you can remember the Busby Babes, the chances are you don't think Beckham is fit to lace Duncan Edwards' boots. If Steve Redgrave is your Olympic hero, then Abrahams and Liddell may seem to belong to a different world – or might have done if *Chariots of Fire* hadn't revived their glory for another generation, a mission the first moments of which Colin Welland recalls in the opening essay of the book.

So this isn't intended as a definitive list of any sort. Rather, it's a series of vibrant writings from a cross-section of the sporting community and beyond, celebrating all aspects of British sport and the people who play it, while recalling moments when they, like a six-year-old boy under the covers one unforgettable night in the 1960s, wanted to shout 'Come and listen to this!'

'And Clay is down. Clay is down…'

Abrahams' and Liddell's 1924 Olympic victories
Colin Welland

They were standing, grinning, arm-in-arm, not knowing what to do with themselves, posing before a moving picture camera for, no doubt, the first time in their lives. The year was 1924. They were athletes pausing in training. Their names were Abrahams and Liddell.

Sitting before an editing machine in the bowels of the National Film Archive, I looked them straight in the eye. I was about to write a film about their exploits, which then, in 1980, were largely forgotten. Presenting these men to the world again was a huge responsibility. They were, you could say, at my mercy. 'Don't worry, boys,' I said. 'I'll try to make a good job of it!'

For they were, indeed, two truly remarkable characters. Not only fine runners – world-beaters, in fact – but individuals with the courage and self-belief both to defeat their opponents on the track and to challenge the forces of prejudice and cant which threatened to scotch their burgeoning athletic careers before they'd even started.

Of the two Eric Liddell was, at first sight, the most appealing – in some ways an uncomplicated soul, with a clear-cut, simple Christian faith, a forthright and total honesty, and an almost bull-like strength to hurl himself around a track faster than any man on earth. His church suspected self-glorification; to him, he ran for the glory of God. If he sounds a bit of a pain in the neck, who carried his evangelism before him like a protest banner, he wasn't. Far from it. Of all the people I talked to who knew him, from none did I hear a word against. He was a gentle charmer who sped like a bullet. After running, he'd often step up his ladder and state his beliefs to the cheering crowds. Because of who he was, folk listened – and he was good at it. For that was what he was destined to be – a missionary – and he missioned as well as he ran. The battle was between the two. And for the moment running was winning, for which we can *all* give thanks.

Harold Abrahams, on the other hand, was far more involved. A moody, some would say chip-on-the-shoulder type, who believed that he could be the fastest man alive once he'd struggled through and free of the antisemitism which ran rife all about him. It dogged, he believed – and with some justification – his every step as he struggled upward and onward towards fulfilling his intense, even fiery, ambition to leave the world's swiftest sprinters in his wake.

On the one occasion the two athletes met head on, at the British Championships at Stamford Bridge, Liddell nosed in front, and Abrahams was distraught. Not having Liddell's inner strength, he crumbled, his certainty of his own ultimate success stuttered and staggered. It took the foresight of a certain Sam Mussabini, half-Arab, half-Italian, to

Liddell beats Abrahams to the tape in a scene from Chariots of Fire, *scripted by Colin Welland*

see the real potential in the Jewish Harold. He set about 'getting that extra yard', not through exhortation, but by technique. Whereas Liddell was charged with passion and sheer inborn strength, Mussabini honed Abrahams into a veritable running machine.

By the time they stepped out onto the track at the Paris Olympic Games of 1924, they had both left many struggles behind them, all of them won – on Abrahams' side by a sheer dogged determination, fostered by the brilliant Mussabini, himself banned from the Games by bureaucratic lunacy; and in Liddell's case by a sublime certainty in the spiritual worthiness of his efforts, bolstered by a natural speed which must indeed have been God-given.

In the short sprint – then as now the Blue Riband of the Games – Abrahams was fortunate not to have to face his powerful Scottish teammate. For Liddell had remained true to his beliefs and pulled out of the hundred's heats because they were run on a Sunday. But the Englishman still had a formidable field arrayed against him: world record-holder Charlie Paddock – the Californian Cannonball – and New York thunderbolt Jackson Scholtz, barely fractions of a second behind Charlie on his recently recorded times. Seated in exile in his hotel near the stadium, Mussabini silently re-mouthed his instructions: 'Wait for the gun, and then release. Only then: the gun – release!' And Abrahams did, springing from the line and hurling himself down the cinder track to snatch the coveted Gold and glory. First to greet him beyond the tape was Liddell, generously and genuinely rejoicing in his friend's victory.

His task was perhaps even more daunting than Abrahams'. Out of the sprint, he'd plumped for the quarter, a distance he'd barely run before. Around him was gathered the usual galaxy of Yankee stars, their jaws dropping when he wished them all, in turn, the best of success. Recognising him as something special, an American coach passed a note into his hand. It read: 'He that honoureth me, I will honour.' With this biblical text in his grasp, Eric Liddell ran the race of his life. Head back and arms flailing, he powered his way magnificently into history.

He never ran competitively again. He'd served his God with his speed as he'd always intended. Now he could return to the more practical service he'd been born into. As a missionary in China, he died under Japanese occupation, barely into his forties.

Abrahams, on the other hand, ever the pragmatist, gave up his battle with the English establishment and joined it instead. After one more Olympics he converted to Christianity to marry the love of his life, and went on to become a distinguished broadcaster with the BBC. And – certainly in those days – you couldn't get more establishment than that.

Two men, two winners, two contrasting spirits. They're remembered now. They deserve never to be forgotten.

The Alpine Club
Fergus Fleming

'The sporting passion exists to a greater or lesser degree, in some shape or other, in the breast of every genuine British man.' Thus spake *Blackwood's Magazine* in the summer of 1859, and an admirable sentiment it was too. The Victorian idea of sport, however, was not quite the same as our own. According to *Blackwood's*, sport was 'physical exercise combined with hazard', which meant, primarily, fox-hunting or, at a pinch, tiger-shooting and buffalo-stalking. But these, as *Blackwood's* conceded, were élitist pursuits. A new activity was needed, one that satisfied the 'national urge' yet was open to all classes. It was pleased, therefore, to announce that 'The great discovery of the day is a species of sport to which its devotees give the not unapt name of Mountaineering'.

Britain's love-affair with mountains – with the Alps, specifically – had been gestating since the dawn of the nineteenth century. Poets, painters, scientists and tourists had been intrigued by the Alps; so too had a growing body of daredevils who (many found this incredible) actually enjoyed climbing the things. Initially a sport that dared not speak its name, mountaineering gained in popularity and by the 1850s it could no longer be suppressed. On 22 December 1857 a small group of enthusiasts gathered in Astley's Hotel, Covent Garden, to create the Alpine Club.

At its inception the Alpine Club's aims were modest: twice-yearly dinners over which members could swap stories, and maybe a journal in which these stories could be published. Its constitution was 'the promotion of good fellowship amongst mountaineers, of mountain climbing and mountain exploration throughout the world, and of better knowledge of the mountains through literature, science and art'. Critics railed against the Alpine Club: it was a malevolent institution, which encouraged the nation's youth to risk life and limb in the pointless pursuit of height. They were wasting their breath. Everyone, it seemed, wanted to become an Alpine sportsman. The attraction was plain: thanks to steam locomotion, Europe's highest – and arguably most beautiful – mountains could be attained from London within a few days. Those who boarded the train were guaranteed much hazard and plentiful exercise in a bracing climate. And best of all, the Alps were not just mountains: they were an uncharted wilderness in which a Victorian man could make his mark.

Britons were not intrinsically better mountaineers than anyone else – though they should have been, for the British Isles contained excellent rock climbing; it was rather that their country was wealthier and politically more stable than those in continental Europe. Its inhabitants, therefore, had the money and the leisure to indulge their sporting whims. (Almost half the Alpine Club were well-paid middle-class professionals who enjoyed long summer holidays.) There was, too, an imperialist urge to which Britons were particularly susceptible. They were accustomed to conquest; the Alps needed to be conquered; and so they went there.

During the 1850s and 1860s British mountaineers swept through the Alps in an orgy of discovery. One by one – sometimes in great clusters – the unclimbed peaks fell to the Union Jack. The period has been dubbed the Golden Age of Mountaineering and one can see why, for the Alpine Clubbers not only vanquished Europe's highest peaks but did so with no equipment whatsoever. Their high-altitude wear comprised a thin flannel suit. Sometimes they stooped to crampons, but generally they relied on a good set of hobnails. Ice-axes had yet to be invented and they hacked steps with hatchets of the sort used for splitting kindling. Their main standby was the alpenstock, an unwieldy pole measuring six feet or more. In extremis, they might deploy a ladder.

They were an eclectic bunch, these climbers of the Golden Age. The Alpine Club embraced every branch of society, from barristers to bricklayers: one man had been a spy for the Tsar, another a cowboy; an extraordinarily versatile member listed himself as musician, artist, actor, cricketer and skater, on top of which he was also a soldier, Conservative MP and Master of Lunacy. And there was one who was a printer's apprentice from Southwark. His name was Edward Whymper.

Possessed of extraordinary fitness and determination, Whymper was Britain's predominant mountaineer. In training at home he might walk thirty miles per day. In the Alps he was capable of outstanding feats of endurance: during one eighteen-day odyssey he climbed more than 100,000 feet of rock and ice. Nobody could match his ability. He dominated the Golden Age and it was fitting, therefore, that he brought it to a close.

By 1865 practically every Alpine peak had been climbed. But the Matterhorn remained inviolate. A pyramid of rock that towered over the Swiss village of Zermatt, the mountain had withstood countless assaults. Most experts deemed it unclimbable. In July 1865 Whymper proved the experts wrong. Blazing a new and apparently impossible route, he at last reached the summit – garnishing his victory with the defeat of an Italian team who were racing him from the other side. But his triumph was short-lived. A rope snapped during the descent, sending four of Whymper's seven-strong party to their deaths. After a 4,000-foot plummet their remains were barely recognisable. (A Reuters report contained such hideous descriptions that it had to be suppressed.) It became the world's most famous climbing disaster. The Golden Age never recovered from it. Neither did Whymper. He abandoned his Alpine career and spent the rest of his life lecturing on that last, notorious climb. Some thought him a hero, but, haunted by nightmares and by rumours that he – or someone – had cut the rope, Whymper grew grimmer by the year. Finally, in 1911, he booked into a Chamonix hotel, locked his door and then, quietly, he died.

The Alpine Club outlived both Whymper and his reputation. Despite a request from Queen Victoria that mountaineering be abolished, the club continued to thrive. Exporting the skills they had acquired in the Alps, its members moved to mountains farther afield – to the Caucasus, the Rockies, the Andes, the Pamirs and the Himalayas – clocking up an impressive list of ascents. During the twentieth century, their exploits were equalled (and

The First Ascent of the Matterhorn *by Gustave Doré: Whymper and his team reach the summit*

often superseded) by mountaineers from other nations. Yet when Everest was first conquered in 1953 it was a British team that struggled to the summit. As images of Edmund Hillary and Tenzing Norgay clattered off the presses, many could only marvel at the appropriateness of their achievement. It had been a hundred years since Britons first donned their tackety boots and sprang up an Alp; now their spiritual descendants were standing on top of the world.

Fifty years after Everest, Britain is no longer the monopolistic player it once was. But it still commands respect in the mountaineering fraternity. There are Swiss, German, Austrian, Italian, American and Polish Alpine Clubs. But nobody ever speaks of a British Alpine Club. It is, without question, *the* Alpine Club.

Royal Ascot
Dick Francis

According to Noël Coward, only mad dogs and Englishmen go out in the midday sun. Which must be why, when the sun is at its highest and the days are long and steamy, thousands and thousands of Englishmen tog themselves in thick, black, hot and heavy morning coats to wind their way through the traffic-choked country roads of eastern Berkshire to *the* event of 'the season' – Royal Ascot. A four-day horse-racing festival where the great and the good, the less great and the downright bad, congregate at the sovereign's racecourse to eat and to drink, to win and to lose, but, most importantly, to see and to be seen.

It is fitting that the first race on the Tuesday, the opening day, is called the Queen Anne Stakes, for it was Queen Anne who decided, whilst out riding in Windsor Great Park in 1711, that a course be laid for the racing of horses near the village of East Cote, now Ascot. The land was purchased for the then princely sum of £558 and the first races were held later the same year in the presence of the Queen and her Court. With the open carriage procession much as it remains to this day, the first four-day Royal Ascot meeting occurred in 1720 during the reign of George I, a welcome distraction from the South Sea Bubble crisis of the time.

The annual four days of the Royal Meeting were the only racing on the course until 1945, but since then the number of days has grown to twenty-five, including nine of steeple-chasing. However, it is still the Royal Ascot days that are the finest. Each has six races, all of them top flight, with the best flat-racing horses in the world competing for the highest prizes. From the Windsor Castle Stakes for the two-year-old babies, who sprint just five furlongs, to the Gold Cup, a two-and-a-half mile endurance test for horses over four, the racing is superb.

The horses' coats glisten in the sun, the featherweight jockeys in their brilliant silks are tossed like dander onto stamp-sized saddles, the cream of Thoroughbreds canter over the lush green turf past the crowded grandstand on the way to the start: all is ready for the fray. The Queen is in her seat, the horses are in the stalls, the flag is up. They're off. A sea of eyes swivels to catch a glimpse of straining muscles and stretched tendons. A roar begins to swell as, neck and neck, nostril to nostril, the equine stars battle for supremacy. 'Move yer blooming arse,' shouts Eliza Doolittle in *My Fair Lady* (did you notice in the film that the horses race past the stands in the wrong direction?). Nowadays, some of the calls of encouragement from the Silver Ring are less polite, albeit as precisely to the point, as a kaleidoscopic mass flashes past the post, the winner to be decided by the judge with his slow-motion action replay. 'Photograph, photograph!'

But to say that Royal Ascot is solely about the racing is like claiming that Christmas dinner is just about eating turkey. What about the stuffing and the gravy, the roasted chestnuts and the cranberry sauce, the mince pies and the sweetmeats, the pudding and the brandy butter? To savour only the racing at Ascot is to miss out on the tastiest morsels.

Royal Ascot is synonymous with fashion in general and hats in particular. The dress code for the Royal Enclosure states that ladies must wear a hat which covers the crown of the head. Fortunately, this allows a degree of latitude expertly exploited by London's milliners, with feathers always in abundance. Four days, four hats, four outfits, with shoes and bags to match, ensure it is an expensive week and one for which the planning starts as soon as the previous meeting is over. To be shown on the television or pictured for the *Tatler* in last year's creation has to be avoided whatever the cost. Notwithstanding that their suits are inappropriate for the summer solstice, the men are lucky that they do not face the annual *haute couture* challenge of choosing between a Chanel or a Gucci, a Giorgio Armani or a Louis Vuitton, a Jean Paul Gaultier or an Yves Saint Laurent. But striped or spotted tie? Grey or black top hat? Decisions, decisions.

Picnics were invented for Royal Ascot. Numbered spaces in Car Park 1 are passed down from father to son and it is here that the art of the picnic is taken to new extremes. Champagne and smoked salmon are *de rigueur*, whilst crystal glasses, best china, dining table, armchairs, silver candelabra and a butler are no less expected. It is a game of two halves. Act One commences early as the players congregate for lunch anytime after ten. An adjournment from the feast is made promptly at a quarter to two for the Royal Procession and the sports. Following the last race, with fresh delights and chilled white wines, the second sitting begins and may continue until after dark, which is pretty late in England during June. And there is always tomorrow.

The racing is magnificent, the fashions are spectacular and the picnics may be delicious, but the real stars of the Royal Ascot meeting are the gate-men. Lounge-suited and bowler-hatted, they can spot an illegal entrant at a hundred paces. As the massed crowds surge through narrow openings, they pluck out the miscreants and unceremoniously boot them back to their proper place. It is not an easy task, for there are two categories who wear no badges: those trying to get a shifty break and, of course, the Royal Family.

I haven't mentioned the dirty packed race trains from Waterloo, the struggle to get a seat in the stands, the queues for the loos, the drunks lying around under the trees near the paddock, the shoving and the pushing, the beer-sticky floors in the bars, the raucous inebriated singing around the bandstand or, indeed, the traffic jams to get both into and out of the racecourse. There are some delights that need to be experienced directly to understand the true flavour of a day at the races. Then there are the all too frequent days in an English summer when the weather does not perform according to the script. But, like a childhood memory, all Royal Ascot days are sunny days.

Overleaf: *'Come on, Dover, move yer bloomin' arse!' yells Eliza in the Ascot scene from* My Fair Lady

Badminton horse trials
Ginny Elliot

Mention the name Badminton and the pulse quickens. Foot-and-mouth restrictions may have wiped out the 2001 event, but nothing else will erase memories of the 'home' of eventing. Badminton is to three-day eventing as Wimbledon is to tennis, Lord's to cricket and Ascot to racing. Whether you are rider or spectator, the place to be in the first week of May is on the Duke of Beaufort's spectacular Gloucestershire estate. The world's best three-day event riders will be competing in the year's first four-star event and the crowds will again flock to witness the drama and the glory of one of the most fearsome cross-country courses in existence.

The 10th Duke of Beaufort commissioned Colonel Trevor Horn to design and build a course to give riders experience of a decent track and fences before the Olympics. The first event to be held in the stunning parkland setting of Badminton House was in 1949, when approximately 10,000 people watched the cross-country. It would have surprised many that this annual gathering would grow to be one of the largest spectator events in the world. Second only to the Indy 500 motor extravaganza, Badminton now has more than 250,000 visitors over the three days of competition. Riders at that first event would have paid only £2 to enter and the winner walked away with £150. This wouldn't even cover today's entry fee of £210, let alone the first prize of £27,500. The number of starters has grown from around twenty-five in the early days to over a hundred today. Some would say that this is the price for professionalism in the sport, but anyone standing by the 'ten minute halt area' would quickly realise that competitors in this perilous sport have retained the Corinthian spirit of days gone by. Riders who have already completed the course will freely give advice and encouragement to those still to set out on the test of nerves and skill, where thirty fences are designed to challenge the most fearless and athletic of equine contestants.

Eventing is practically unique in that men and women compete on level terms. This was not always the case, for it was not until the mid-1950s that women were allowed to enter international events. Margaret Hough paved the way with a Badminton victory on Bambi in 1954. Since then, the ladies have held their own, with Sheila Wilcox winning in three consecutive years and Lucinda Green leading all riders with six wins. Surprisingly, mares have only won on three occasions and never since 1960. Badminton has made heroes of men, women and horses alike. Jane Bullen rode the diminutive Our Nobby to victory despite the horse being only fifteen hands tall, while Richard Walker won at the tender age of eighteen. Riders from all around the world and every walk of life have competed, from the present Duke of Beaufort (who finished second in 1959) to the

Ginny Elliot (as Ginny Leng) on Welton Houdini at Badminton, May 1993

indomitable Australian Bill Roycroft, who rode Stoney Crossing to finish placed at Badminton, in the Cheltenham Gold Cup and in the Foxhunters at Aintree – all in the space of one month!

Dreams or nightmares of Badminton must fill millions of sleeping hours, for every aspiring event rider claims that their ambition is to ride over the Badminton fences. If dreams come to reality and these riders make the required grade, then most days of late winter and early spring are focused on getting both horse and rider mentally and physically prepared for the first major test of the season. This is no easy task, for the multi-disciplined requirements of eventing are the equestrian equivalent of the pentathlon. Horse and rider must combine the athletic skills required of dressage and the accuracy of show jumping, yet still retain the bravery and stamina for the cross-country elements. The Badminton test is probably the most severe of the year, as there has been little time for the horse and rider partnership to iron out early-season problems before entering the pressure cauldron of the Badminton parkland. It is perhaps this early position in the eventing calendar that maintains Badminton's continued prominence in everybody's mind. Badminton is the first major event of the year for riders who have achieved the required experience to ride in four-star competition. They have probably been through a four-year graduation and a strict qualification schedule to get there, so nerves are taut at the thought of blowing months of training. These riders have the added pressure of the fact that Badminton is the recognised proving-ground for Olympic, European or World Championship selection, with those competitions always taking place in late summer. The more established riders have their own pressures in that Badminton provides their first opportunity to prove inexperienced horses in four-star company. The size of the crowds, the intensity of noise and the presence of television cameras are experiences that young horses are unlikely to have encountered at lesser events. A good introduction here could be the making of a future equine star and a passport to further glory.

Much of the success of Badminton is due to Colonel Frank Weldon, who was the course designer from 1968 to 1988. His successor Hugh Thomas has overseen the course-building and development of this unique event for the past thirteen years and has maintained the rich Badminton traditions, while quietly ensuring customer satisfaction for spectators, television viewers and competitors. This is not an easy formula to juggle. The public demands excitement and spectacle for their money, which is desperately needed for the continuance of the discipline. The Badminton fences have remained a proper test for the best of the best, while their construction and the setting have ensured spectacular viewing. The Lake fences have huge audience appeal and the backdrop of Badminton House makes this a unique venue for competitors and spectators alike.

Badminton is a delight for all concerned. Competitors and their grooms enjoy the excellent facilities and camaraderie of the horsebox park, with the Thursday night drinks party in Badminton House featuring as the main social event for owners, officials and riders. Visiting event enthusiasts not only have close-up viewing of the thrills and spills of the three days' action; they can also turn their attention to the largest shopping mall of trade stands at any country fair in England. Whether it be T-shirt hot or oilskin wet, their enthusiasm is never dented. Even those not able to be there in person are well catered for, with BBC coverage getting excellent audience figures. For those even further afield, the arrival of the internet has enabled followers to keep tabs on the action worldwide. At the 2000 event, more than 135,000 downloads of the daily highlights were recorded on the Badminton website.

No matter who leads the traditional laps of honour around the packed arena and collects the spectacular trophy of three silver horses and riders, the real winner will be Badminton itself, whose name will endure long after the equine and human celebrities are forgotten.

Becks: *the David Beckham phenomenon*
Sue Mott

You could reasonably argue that the market positioning of David Beckham is not far removed from that of Christ. Soft-eyed, pacific, iconic, arms spreadeagled along the cross of St George: those were the *bon voyage* pictures of Britain's most famous man as he prepared for the global attrition of the 2002 World Cup in the Far East.

Don't tell us it was a coincidence. Beckham's image – which became a tradeable commodity in his negotiations with Manchester United in the spring of 2002 – had emerged as an international brand as powerful and instantly recognisable as Pepsi. It was an extraordinary concept. Once missionaries had taken the word of God into far-flung corners of the earth. Now marketeers take pictures of Beckham.

How could this happen to a sweet-faced boy, the son of a gas-fitter's mate and a hairdresser, who scored over a hundred goals in three seasons for Ridgeway Rovers in the Enfield District League? Beckham's talent was not accidental. It was a devotedly honed skill, which made it all the more appreciated – and far less fleeting – than the mercurial gifts of a George Best had been. It became of matter of myth that his father, Ted, would spend endless hours on some park pitch in Leytonstone, East London, coaxing his middle son to near-perfection on the ball.

And young David was eminently coachable. He laboured on, spurning parties, drink, girls and the other understandable distractions of youth. His reward was heavenly. He was watching *Blue Peter* at the age of eleven when a feature on Bobby Charlton's Soccer Skills tournament was broadcast. He entered and won, with the highest ever total score. More to the point, the event was held at Old Trafford, sacred home of Manchester United. 'There was no other club for me,' he said later. At the age of fourteen, he signed for them.

If the building blocks of global notoriety were even then within his grasp, by the time he reached manhood Beckham was playing a game that had become the secular religion. With its high masses of scarves and songs and ecstatic togetherness, it resembled a church service at the Roman Coliseum. Becks was the beautiful gladiator and was worshipped accordingly.

Turn the other cheek, said the Lord. Love one another. And he didn't just mean Posh Spice. But there wasn't much love in evidence that evening in France when the younger Beckham's leg flicked upwards in spiteful retaliation during the 1998 World Cup against Argentina. Diego Simeone collapsed to the ground and simulated a death scene from *Reservoir Dogs*. Beckham was sent off, disgraced. We lost.

Afterwards only Tony Adams, the former England captain, spoke to him. He walked across the dressing room to tell the tracksuited lad with his head in his hands that he was a great player and that Adams loved him to bits. Alan Shearer, sitting next to him, said nothing. Beckham uttered only one word: 'Sorry.'

In the hysterical aftermath, his family was besieged, his effigies were hung, he was all but ritually disembowelled. Lesser mortals would have crumbled. But Beckham was developing a temperament that has stillness and peace at its core. He played superbly the following season, and respect for his calmness and maturity in the face of a storm was instilled in the wider watching public. He had revealed an Achilles heel and then set it in the plaster of his own will. Admiration intensified.

Like Madonna – this time *not* the biblical version – he likes to play with his image. He is undeniably pretty. He is a gay icon alongside Shirley Bassey, and though they do not share a similar taste in frocks, one of the most notorious moments in his life remains the night he went out in a sarong. When football supporters, not generally the most tolerant of beasts, are content to see their midfielders in a skirt, it's clear that all human life is evolving around the tastes of a single trendsetter.

Marriage to a pop star was perhaps inevitable. But Victoria Beckham, *neé* Posh, was never merely a pretty accoutrement on the arm, like a Louis Vuitton handbag. Even Beckham saw the funny side. 'Blonde and quiet' was how he liked his women; Victoria, he was forced to admit, was 'dark and loud'. Their wedding is largely remembered for enormous purple thrones, wandering swans and a tendency to overdo it in kids' dressing-up clothes that make you either gasp with horror or sigh with indulgence. Their baby son, Brooklyn, looked like a little Caligula in a crown of woven leaves.

But time heals wounds, even those perpetrated by *OK!* magazine. Beckham's dignity in the face of vile abuse against his wife and child at football matches was remarkable. Once he raised a finger; other men would have raised a chainsaw. He had his enemies, but he came through it all. By the time England were vying to qualify for the 2002 World Cup, he was captain. The choice was controversial. He might have been too young, too inarticulate, too unworldly to offer true leadership on the pitch. On the other hand, he had respect and ability and a guaranteed place in the team. Sven-Göran Eriksson, England's new manager, took a Swedish view of the captaincy. Sex rules. And Beckham was sexier than the rest.

Beckham's elevation to England's leading man – England the country, not merely the team that plays football – was cemented when he scored the winning goal in the climactic first-round match against Argentina. But his coolness in taking that penalty did more than secure England a place in the second round. It also redeemed Beckham himself, if any further redemption were needed, from the memory of that other confrontation with Argentina four years earlier. The circle had been closed.

Because in the end, everybody likes him. He is good, rich, kind, loyal, and can bend the ball round an eight-man wall. He is masculine and feminine. He looks good in a vest and a skirt (though not necessarily at the same time). He has moved our culture along. Maybe not quite as far as Christ did, but at least in a forward direction.

David Beckham celebrates his goal against Greece which clinched England's entry into the 2002 World Cup

Bev: the genius of Brian Bevan
Colin Welland

Ball out, ball out!
Hear supporters call.
Scrum-half, stand off,
Centres pass the ball.
It goes to Knowelden,
He's a bold'un,
Albert Pimblett hears the call!
Sling it out to Bevan
He's the man to beat them all!

Uncle Don had come all the way from Liverpool especially to see him. A lifelong Anfield devotee, he'd wearied at the praises we'd heaped on our hero, my Dad and I, and had trekked into Rugby League territory, squashed between his city and Manchester, to see the phenomenon for himself.

My family had moved into the hinterland of Liverpool after the May blitzes of 1941, and we'd settled in to live among the 'Woolybacks', as Scousers call true Lancastrians. At the war's end we were introduced to and quickly seduced by the sheer exhilaration of the thirteen-a-side game. Amazing really, because Evertonian Dad was a Toffee Blue through and through. But once bitten there's no going back. Warrington, now our team, trotted out to the stirring bars of 'Entry of the Gladiators'. Don's jaw dropped: 'Is that him? You must be bloody joking!'

He certainly looked a bit of a joke, our Brian Bevan, the greatest try-scorer the game has ever known. Bald, toothless, wracked with a smoker's cough, he strode the park on spindly, bandaged knees and feet splayed like a chicken's. But give him the ball…! He's the only player of any code – and I include them all, from soccer to gridiron, Union to Gaelic, even Aussie rules – who, on his taking possession, could cause every stand to leap to its feet. For wherever, whenever, for whatever he'd stepped into his stride, something magical would happen.

For a schoolboy's hero he simply didn't fit the bill. In his twenties he looked fifty. For an Australian by birth he looked every inch an *un*athlete. Yet his pictures adorned my bedroom walls, and his was the name bandied about with pride in our Monday morning playground inquests.

Why? Well, his opponents' supporters laughed and jeered when he scuttled under the desperate weight of a multi-tackle … out of sheer relief. They laughed in terror when he

In a league of his own: Brian Bevan in 1952

stuttered into his loping stride, mouth gaping, head arched back like a frightened kangaroo, and left his flailing hunters standing. His speed was phenomenal, his sidestep dual-carriageway, his change of pace as devastating as it was imperceptible. I can't remember the number of times I saw him score six tries in a match – and I mean tries from *anywhere*.

Once, facing a Wigan side totally composed of internationals, he was given the ball on the blind side of a scrum, on his *own* line. Twenty seconds later he was touching down in Wigan's opposite corner, having left some of the game's most illustrious names grasping at thin air. Oh, the ecstasy of it – the sheer screaming ecstasy of it. People talk about the majesty of Gareth Edwards' much-lauded Barbarians try. Bevan gave it to us regally every week!

Ask the game's greats who played against him. I did. 'What was it like to tackle him?' I enquired of that fine Welsh full-back, Glyn Moses. 'I dunno,' he said. 'I never laid a bloody finger on him!' Billy Boston – now there's another name to conjure with – tells me he only played against Bev the odd time, their careers barely overlapping. On the first occasion, he'd heard all about the toothless wonder and was determined to make his presence felt. It was planned to kick the ball to Bev at the start, with Billy following up speedily to give him what for. 'Perfect kick,' remembers the Welsh wizard, 'and I caught him in my sights. I launched… but he wasn't there! The crowd laughed as he strode off upfield, leaving me flat on my face for dead. But I didn't mind. Better men than me, I thought…'

True enough. Picture Wilderspool Stadium on a cold, frosty winter's day. The pitch had been under straw, and piles of it littered the touchlines. We were playing Workington in the Cup, a Workington led from the back by another Welsh wizard, the fine Gus Risman. His team were leading with ten minutes to go. Our only hope was the Bev. True to form, he took the ball down his wing in full flight. Workington scrambled desperately and in vain to reach him. All save Gus, who was loping confidently to cut him off, angles absolute, trajectory perfect – just a matter of time. That time reached, the master full-back pitched himself into the tackle… into thin air. For Bev had stepped into overdrive on Gus' commitment, and was touching down between the posts. 'Look at Gus!' my Dad said. And I did. The great man was sitting covered in straw, shaking his head and applauding. He too knew there was no shame in being beaten by the best.

Bev played on for fifteen years for Warrington, then for a couple or so for Blackpool. In the process he scored nearly 800 tries – a record which even the great Billy himself couldn't hope to emulate. When Bevan died a few years ago, I was honoured to be invited by a proud Warrington Council to share with his widow the unveiling of his statue. It's a magnificent work, unlike so many coarse and clumsy sporting 'tributes'. His figure, in bronze, flies high, in full stride, above the Warrington traffic. Before I spoke, his widow whispered, 'Don't mention his teeth, Colin – I asked the artist to put them back in!' And sure enough, up there is Bev as I never saw him, resplendent with a full set – not the gums-agape gazelle I fondly remember. But no matter. Teeth or no teeth, Bev's record speaks for itself – and for once, glorious, glowing memories are more than enough.

Ian Botham's 1981 Test season
Frank Keating

The year 1981 did not begin auspiciously for the young England cricket captain Ian Botham. In the first week of January, the twenty-five-year-old angling enthusiast went fishing in Ireland and hardly caught a tiddler. In the second week, he appeared before Scunthorpe magistrates charged with common assault following a Christmas party incident outside Tiffany's nightclub in the town. He elected to go to trial in April because, by the third week of January, he had flown with his England team to the Caribbean for a Test match series against Clive Lloyd's West Indies, probably the most irresistibly relentless international cricket side since Don Bradman's 1948 Australians. By his return in April – when he was completely exonerated of all charges at Grimsby Crown Court – Botham was facing a different prosecution in the public prints, one which questioned his capabilities even as a Test match player, and certainly as a Test match captain.

The series in the West Indies had not only been predictably lost on the field, but beset with traumas off it – not least expulsion from Guyana for reasons related to South Africa's apartheid, the loss through injury of dependable vice-captain and opening bowler Bob Willis, and the harrowingly sudden death of the England coach and Botham soulmate Ken Barrington. Botham's leadership had been typically breezy in adversity, but with no Willis or Barrington to consult it was essentially too haphazard and off-the-cuff. Even those of us fellow-travellers enamoured of such a dynamic and bonny breath-of-fresh-air cricketer were, as we gathered around his captain's perk (a fridge in his hotel room) on those tropical nights, already counselling resignation from the captaincy, insisting his versatile cricketing grandeur was suffering, dependent as it was on instinct at the crease, not cautious calculation in the pavilion or public relations. The great bear of a boy would have none of it, of course – but his intrepid self-confidence was to be dented at once when the selectors nominated him as captain for only the first two Tests of the upcoming Ashes series against the Australians, in effect putting him on public trial.

So with Botham as well as the England team insecure, both made a slack and sorry start to the summer. The first Test at Nottingham was miserably lost, the second at Lord's pallidly drawn, and there, when Botham marched back, seething, through an unchivalrously admonishing pin-drop silence in the Long Room after his second nought of the match, there was no doubt it would be his last as captain. Mike Brearley, who had enthusiastically championed the young prince's succession, reluctantly agreed to return.

The evidence was striking: before being made captain, Somerset's bold baron Beefy had, in only twenty-five Tests, begun to rip up records with audacious, carefree dash – 1,300 runs at 40 with six centuries, bucketfuls of daredevil catches, and 140 wickets at 19 apiece. In his ten Tests as captain (all, cruelly, against mighty West Indies) he had scored just 242 runs at a miserable 14, and taken 29 wickets at a costly 34. No contest. It was already mid-July, and the year of Botham's comeuppance (as his enemies had it) was already forlorn enough for friends to suggest a summer recharging his batteries on the humdrum county ground at Taunton and in the surrounding pastoral pubs – an opportunity the sympathetic Brearley offered when the team gathered for the third Test at Leeds. 'I'll quite understand if you don't want to play,' said Brearley. 'No bloody fear,' said Beefy, 'these Aussies are there for the taking.' Brearley smiled a weak, unconvinced, psychotherapist's smile. Similar realistic pessimism continued to hang over Headingley as heavily as its pewtery grey skies while Australia batted on, nonchalantly to declare at 401. Then they skittled England for a feeble 174 (Botham's 50 the only defiance). By Saturday night's close at the end of the third day, England, following on, were a squirming 6 for 1 and obvious humiliation postponed for a day because they still did not play Tests on the Sabbath.

Although he played for Somerset, Botham lived in Yorkshire, in the village of Epworth, and that Saturday night he and his wife Kath had organised a barbecue there for both teams and a few trusted friends. The Australians enjoyed it, presumptive and gloating; by Monday evening at the latest they would be 2–0 up and the Ashes surely regained. The Englishmen partied as at a wake, a number of them mournfully drowning the likelihood that this would be their final Test match. For both reasons a great deal of drink was consumed. As befits a good host, Botham was last to bed. It was way past dawn.

Epworth may have been the birthplace of John Wesley, but there was no hint of any inspired English revivalism by teatime on Monday when England stood at 135 for 7, still needing 92 to avoid the shamefaced innings defeat. With two hours' play left that evening when tail-ender Graham Dilley joined Botham at the wicket, the England team had been booked out of their hotel and the Headingley caterers, stewards and gatekeepers stood down for next day. Botham greeted Dilley at the crease: 'Let's go down in a blaze: just play your shots, let's enjoy it.' Enjoy it they did: with some joyously uncomplicated slogging they added 117 in an hour and ten minutes. Then Chris Old and Botham put on 67. Astonishingly, England were 124 ahead at the close, with one wicket standing, Botham a valiantly outrageous and undefeated 145. Unforgettable, and almost operatic in its resonant boldness. Revivalism all right, but surely not enough?

Willis was out at once next morning – Botham still undefeated for 149 (26 merry fours and a six into the hot-dog stall). The nation was enthralled. Yet all auguries insisted that Australia could not lose – just 130 to win on a comfy pitch. Some of the Australians, inveterate gamblers, had even taken the bookmakers' 500–1 against defeat. Inspired by the batting of his comrade Botham, bowler Willis now steamed down the Headingley hill like a demented long-haired valkyrie to pick off the Australians one by one and toss them from the battlefield. They were all out for 111 – Willis a remarkable 8 for 43. The series stood at 1–1. Nine days later, at Edgbaston, roughly the same sort of ravishingly theatrical scenario brought down the curtain on a low-scoring match. This time Australia needed

Ian Botham prepares for his innings at the third Test at Headingley, July 1981

142 to win. On the final evening, in the sunshine, they had unworriedly passed 100 with only four wickets down – when Botham, shirt flapping and grin menacing, grabbed the ball and, cresting the crease like a grand and dauntless shirehorse, shot out five of them for just one run in only 28 balls. Once more unhinged, the infuriated Australians fell 29 runs short. Incredible. England now 2–1 up. More national delirium all round.

Twelve days later, another contest of extraordinary fluctuation at Manchester had Botham again downstage and the utterly decisive lead player, this time with an innings not of last-fling humpety and hooraymanship as at Headingley, but one of majesty and unstoppable conviction. In front of a jam-packed heatwave muster of 20,000 at Old Trafford he hit – and then hit some more – a classical century of unimaginable power and effortless zest. The true-great Oz champion Dennis Lillee was dismissed from his presence with a fusillade of blows which Botham slapped off his eyebrows – six sixes in all, an Ashes record – and cricket-writing's measured sage in *The Times*, John Woodcock, asked on the front page 'Was this the greatest Test innings ever?' In 123 minutes, Botham hit 118. England were to win by 113 runs. The Ashes were retained. And a generally barmy joy was unconfined.

A working-class hero was something to be all right. Between 16 July and 17 August, the former captain who had been reduced to the ranks had not only revived his year, his reputation – to be sure, his place forever in posterity – but had regenerated England's devoted fondness for, and delight in, the glories of cricket itself. When the young Lochinvar with the golden aura had come in through the sunset that penultimate evening at Headingley, the choral-conscious Yorkshire throng had gathered in front of the pavilion and serenaded him with 'Jerusalem'. Following his pyrotechnics with the ball at Edgbaston, they had massed likewise to sing 'Land of Hope and Glory' in raucously unbelieving Brummie accents. After Old Trafford, a writer in the *Guardian* quoted G K Chesterton's approbation of Charles Dickens and pinned it on Botham: 'There is a great man who makes every man feel small. But the really great man is the one who makes every man feel great.'

Nineteen eighty-one ensured Ian Botham everlasting greatness for the sporting pantheon. Just as Botham himself ensured 1981's everlasting greatness for history's.

The British Lions
Eddie Butler

There came a moment on the Lions tour of 2001 when in three cities on the eastern seaboard of Australia hotels were so overbooked, food and drink consumption so vast, attendance records so broken and replica shirt sales so high that the finances of the operation became as important as the sport. Behind the players was marching an extraordinary expeditionary force of support.

A trickle of red die-hards in Perth, far to the west, where the tour began, had become, by sucking in planeloads to Brisbane and Melbourne, a scarlet swarm. By the time of the final Test in Sydney, tens of thousands of fans were making a contribution to commerce measured in tens of millions of dollars. It was support on a macro-economic scale.

But it was not worth a pinch of salt compared with what was about to happen on the field of play. Grand-scale money-matters were about to be rendered worthless.

The bruised and battered tourists had already set new records of their own in their three-Test series against the world champion Wallabies. They had won by a mile in Brisbane, had lost by a wide margin in Melbourne and now found themselves in the Olympic Stadium for the decider. The showdown was going the way of the Australian side, who had always pledged that they would be at their best in Sydney.

The Lions trailed 23–29. But somehow they had found vigour in their weary limbs and had rallied for one final assault. A penalty kick to the corner had set up a line-out five metres from the Wallaby try-line. Five tiny metres.

The final scene. The series hung on one throw, one catch and one unspectacular drive. Martin Johnson, a giant as a captain and player, called the ball to himself. Against him was Justin Harrison, winning his first cap in the second row. The totem against the rookie.

Harrison won the ball. Australia cleared their line and survived the final moments. All the bar receipts at Stadium Australia could be added to the ticket returns and the city-wide estimates of expenditure per capita; but this was priceless, this was sport beyond measure.

In 1995, when the sport of rugby union went professional, it was suggested in not always uninformed circles that there would be no place for the Lions. The individual needs of the four countries, England, Ireland, Scotland and Wales, would simply be too intense to allow the best players from each to swan off to the southern hemisphere once every four years.

Two years later the Lions went to South Africa and beat the Springboks 2–1. Six years on, they were still in business. The tour reached that Sydney conclusion and the Lions suffered defeat, but the epic standards of play, which stood in colourful contrast to the spartan tones off the field, as set by New Zealand coach Graham Henry, made the tour even better theatre. For every tale of mutiny against the austere Henry regime – and there were many – there was the sheer brilliance of the rugby, its courage and brutality and verve. The bookings began to be made for New Zealand 2005 even before the dust had settled on the lost tour of 2001.

If 'The Lions are special' became the rather forced mantra of the Henry tour, a Lions trip to New Zealand is specially special. It was here in 1971 that they won their first series of the then modern age. The best of Britain and Ireland had been touring since the late nineteenth century. Their voyages at first were casual gatherings of chums, who packed the dinner jacket first and the boots second. The deck parties on board the steamers drifting southwards lasted as long as an entire modern tour. Only one thing linked the tours of the old days and the jet-stream demands of the new: New Zealand remained the nut that could not be cracked.

The conditions were ideal for the tourists. The All Blacks of the late 1960s had been formidable, but in the early years of the new decade the feeling was growing that they might be past their best. Even the great second row Colin Meads, who had been dazzling and terrorising opponents in equal measure for fourteen years, was, it was whispered when he wasn't around, over the hill.

On the other side, the Lions could not have been more packed with talent, the hard-core of it from Wales, then at the cutting edge of the European game. If Gareth Edwards, J P R Williams, Gerald Davies, Barry John, John Dawes, Mervyn Davies and John Taylor were blue-chip certainties, the one risk the Lions were prepared to take was to entrust the players to the care of Carwyn James. This was no coach of a national team, but of Llanelli. Could the idiosyncratic parish of West Wales become the playing field of four nations?

It could. The Lions drew the final Test, played as always at Eden Park, Auckland, to take the four-match series 2–1. It was a moment of massive significance for the game in the northern hemisphere and it could not have been in greater contrast to the tour of 2001.

In those days the tour would have been followed by a handful of journalists. The Tests survive only as grainy black and white highlights. The few supporters often travelled on the team bus. The players were not spartan in the socio-cultural dimension they brought to their extended stay – twice as long at least as the modern tour – on the other side of the world. Hours spent at local schools, receiving the scrapbooks kept by pupils who adopted them, were only exceeded by time spent in the bar.

The 1974 tour was even more boisterous, if only because hotel sheets in South Africa tended to catch fire more easily than the damp blankets of Invercargill. But the Lions went about their business with even greater purpose on the field. The side, led by Willie John McBride, went through the tour unbeaten and humiliated the isolated Springboks. They ran the South Africans ragged and even managed to win the brawls. This was the golden age of the '99' call. One in, all in.

Brian O'Driscoll of the Lions in action against Western Australia during the 2001 tour

The spirit of the musketeers would probably have lived on and on – who knows how different the rugby order might have remained? – had the Lions managed to keep the momentum going. But in 1977 they returned to New Zealand and lost. The ferocious Lions pack reduced the All Blacks to packing down with three men, but kiwi revenge for '71 was exacted. And it was all slugged out on such bogs and marshes the length of the land in that cold, wet southern winter that defeat was made even more miserable.

And thus was the hegemony of the southern hemisphere re-established. The Lions of 1980 lost in South Africa, the tourists of 1983 and 1993 were beaten by the All Blacks, overwhelmingly in the case of '83. Only a hard-fought 2–1 victory over Australia – playing the Lions in 1989 exclusively for the first time – gave the dying days of the history of amateur rugby a gloss. Until then Australia had merely been a port of call, a warm-up, before the real business of playing New Zealand. By 1989 the Wallabies were worthy of a series in their own right, but even then it was supposed that the World Cup, first played in 1987, would become the highlight of the global game.

It is not clear what happened to change all that. Perhaps the professional game at international level, with its antiseptic sessions behind closed doors, has become remote from its audience. The Lions tour suddenly offered supporters with more leisure time on their hands the chance to find common cause in a pleasant climate.

The supporters of all ages mixed and mingled with a generosity of spirit and purse that was nearly the making of the tour of 2001. But not quite. The players, bruised and battered by their sporting schedule and their ascetic lifestyle, nevertheless proved that nothing compares with the drama on the stage. All they need to do now is relax the absolutism of their austerity and the Lions tour will combine perfectly the social prosperity of the old days and the financial prosperity of the new. And they will win again. As the mantra goes: the Lions are special.

The Busby Babes
Ken Jones

On 1 February 1958 a Manchester United team in the throes of development, excitingly on course to become one of the best English football had ever seen, defeated Arsenal 5–4 at Highbury. Paying alliterative tribute to the vision of Matt Busby, sportswriters had christened them the Busby Babes. It was the last time they would be seen on British soil. Within a week five of the young men who fashioned that thrilling victory were among those who perished in the snow and ice when an aircraft bringing Manchester United home from a European Cup tie against Red Star Belgrade crashed on take-off from Munich. Roger Byrne, David Pegg, Tommy Taylor, Eddie Colman, Billy Whelan and Geoff Bent were killed outright; the man-boy Duncan Edwards, a world star in the making, the youngest player to be capped by England, only twenty-one and already an international on eighteen occasions, had internal injuries, a fractured leg, fractured ribs and severe shock. It was too much even for such a giant. Edwards lingered for fifteen days, raising hopes that he would pull through. Then he died. Busby would recover from grievous injuries, and Bobby Charlton, whose name became synonymous with Manchester United, was among those who survived. But the Babes were no more.

Seen as the flowering of an ideal, the Babes were, in fact, a product of necessity. Returning to civilian life after the Second World War, his playing career clearly over, Busby became manager of Manchester United in October 1945. With no experience, he was in at the deep end. German bombs had wrecked Old Trafford: no stand, no dressing rooms; matches had to be played at Maine Road, home of Manchester City. If these difficulties were not enough for a man coming fresh to management, United were also heavily in debt.

Busby drew strength from the situation. He knew what kind of club he wanted, and there was little remaining of the old one to distract him from his purpose. As Busby would tell the author Arthur Hopcraft, he wanted creative football. He wanted method. 'I wanted to manage the team as I felt players wanted to be managed. To begin with I wanted a more humane approach than there was when I was playing … there never seemed to be enough interest taken in players. The manager was at his desk, and you saw him once a week. From the start I tried to make the smallest member think he was part of the club.'

Importantly – how importantly would be emphasised in the aftermath of Munich – Busby had persuaded a tough former Welsh internationalist half-back, Jimmy Murphy, to work at his side. Impressed by Murphy's passion for the game, Busby was following his instincts. With money in short supply, Murphy's task was to help find and develop young players. 'Jimmy taught me what professional football is all about,' Bobby Charlton would say. 'I remember him dragging me out of practice matches to make a point, and I would stand there, half listening, one eye on the game, eager to get back into it. After a while I realised I would be kept there until Jimmy was satisfied he was getting through.'

Busby's reputation in management quickly grew. Able to draw on a group of mature professional players, and with the shrewd addition of Jimmy Delaney from Celtic, he produced a team that captured the public's imagination. Liverpool won the Championship in that first post-war season, but home and away Manchester United attracted the highest aggregate attendances in the First Division. In 1948 Busby claimed his first trophy when Manchester United brilliantly outplayed Blackpool in the FA Cup final. After finishing second in four of five seasons, United took the League title in 1952.

Busby did not invent the youth policy which became so important to Manchester United's progress; but more than any other manager he put his faith and his reputation into it. The scouting net was cast ever wider, leading in 1953 to the birth of the Babes.

When United lost six of their first eleven games in the 1952–3 season, Busby entered the transfer market to sign the young, combative centre-forward Tommy Taylor from Barnsley, but he knew it was time to gamble on youth. First blooded at outside-left, soon to become a fixture at left-back in the England team, Roger Byrne had already graduated from United's youth academy. Then came Duncan Edwards.

Only sixteen when he made his debut on Easter Monday in 1953, Edwards came to symbolise the Babes. Gifted and strong, he was Murphy's idea of the complete player: 'The best ever,' he said. A month later United won the inaugural FA Youth Cup, trouncing Wolverhampton Wanderers 7–1 in the first leg of the final with a team that included Edwards, Eddie Colman, David Pegg, Liam Whelan and Albert Scanlon – all to become established first team players. At last, English football could see that Busby's optimism was justified.

The flow of talent seemed endless. Mark Jones and Jackie Blanchflower, younger brother of Danny, the famed Tottenham Hotspur and Northern Ireland captain, were soon competing for the centre-half position. And before long United's supporters were introduced to Charlton's immense promise.

The newly fashioned team won their first honour in 1956. Only Johnny Berry and Byrne were left from the 1952 side; only Berry, Taylor and the goalkeeper Ray Wood had been bought. They had won the Championship – eleven points ahead of Blackpool – with an average age of under twenty-three.

In defiance of the Football League, who had forbidden Chelsea to enter a year earlier, Busby went for the European Cup. In the second leg of a first-round tie United put ten goals past Anderlecht at Old Trafford, four of them coming from a local boy, Dennis Viollet, three from the now mature Taylor. They went on to defeat Borussia Dortmund and Atletico Bilbao before losing to Real Madrid in the semi-finals. At the same time they came close to completing the first modern double of League Championship and FA Cup. The Championship was retained with eight points to spare and it did not seem possible that a moderate Aston Villa could stop United at Wembley. A collision between Villa's robust left-winger Peter McParland and the United goalkeeper Ray Wood, which left

Wood with a fractured cheekbone, changed everything. With Blanchflower in goal, United were thrown completely out of gear and lost 2–1.

Setting aside that disappointment, United began the 1957–8 season as expected with five wins and a draw in their opening six games. An unheard-of treble beckoned – the League, the Cup, the European Cup. Then things began to go wrong. Points were dropped everywhere, allowing Wolverhampton Wanderers to pull away. Sensing complacency, Busby made changes and moved to strengthen his defence by signing Northern Ireland's goalkeeper, Harry Gregg, from Doncaster Rovers.

When United set off for Belgrade, defending a two-goal lead from the first leg against Red Star, the team known everywhere as the Busby Babes had perhaps two more years to reach its peak. The horror of Munich prevented us from ever knowing how great it could have been in full maturity.

Matt Busby (in sunglasses) and the Manchester United team take to the air again after the Munich tragedy

Cardiff Arms Park
Alan Watkins

The Cardiff Arms Park took its name from the nearby Cardiff Arms Hotel, long ago demolished. It was in 1874 that sixty-six men paid half-a-crown (12½p) to form the Glamorgan Football (that is, Rugby Union Football) Club. Their first practice was held at the Arms Park, which then sported a cricket pavilion and little else.

The area was subject to periodic flooding from the River Taff, and remained in this perilous condition until its redevelopment as the National Stadium in the 1970s. There was a system of sluices, pipes and taps, but the only man who understood it was dead or had forgotten how it worked. The result was that the ground sometimes resembled a West Wales farmyard, even when it had hardly been raining at all. It was undoubtedly a disgrace, not only to the game of rugby but to the nation.

Nor were the stands and the players' accommodation beneath them any more satisfactory. The favoured building material was corrugated iron in a shade of rusty dark red, supplemented by wood which had clearly seen better days. There were those on the terraces (divided into Field and somewhat superior Enclosure) who claimed they had been spattered with urine from defective plumbing in the pipes above them in the stand. In my visits to the ground in 1946–9 and, less frequently, in the 1950s, I escaped this fate. But I have a clear recollection of the urine trickling down the concrete steps at half-time and, sometimes, during the match itself. Supporters who had been to Twickenham, as many of them had for the England v. Wales match, returned telling of the marvels – the comfortable bars and spacious lavatories – of that dark green stadium in South-West London, like medieval travellers talking about the wonders of Constantinople.

And yet Cardiff Arms Park (the 'the' before the name is optional) was by common consent the greatest rugby ground in the world. To visitors it was as Moscow to Napoleon, while to the Welsh it was a holy place. Dr Danie Craven, who played for South Africa in 1931–8 and was subsequently that country's leading rugby panjandrum, described his experience of the ground:

> It is as if the whole world ... turns against you, and it is useless ever to try and make conversation with a neighbour in the grandstand. Those emotions which Welshmen are known to have are expressed in song, and song based on prayer. How can fifteen opponents on the field pray, and even if they could how can they pray against thousands of vociferous Welshmen?

It was song above all which tended to intimidate the opposition. About an hour before kick-off the band would strike up: a silver as distinct from a brass band, whether from

Bread of heaven: Welsh players look skywards at the newly floodlit Cardiff Arms Park, 1991

Gwaen-cae-Gurwen or the Welch Regiment. After half-an-hour of the stirring marches of J P Sousa (a great favourite in South Wales) it would be time for the singing. It was spontaneous. The band would follow the crowd, who had their own programme: *Aberystwyth* ('Jesu lover of my soul'), *Rachie* (in Welsh), *Diadem* ('All hail the power of Jesus' name'), *Calon Lân* (in Welsh), *Sosban Fach* (in Welsh) and, finally, *Cwm Rhondda* ('Guide me O thou great Jehovah', 'Jehovah' being more authentic than 'Redeemer'), which was once described by the novelist Anthony Powell as the national anthem of South Wales.

Cwm Rhondda alone has survived, the 'Bread of heaven' bit being sung, not at the beginning of matches, but when the Welsh team have scored a try or are doing reasonably well. The decline set in during the 1960s and continued in the new National Stadium during the 1970s. This magnificent structure, holding 72,000 people (and now supplanted – unnecessarily, in my opinion – by the Millennium Stadium) was always popularly known as the Cardiff Arms Park. However, though the standard of singing had diminished, owing to the decline of coal, steel and, above all, chapels, the standard of rugby had improved.

It was the reborn Cardiff Arms Park which saw Wales share the Five (now Six) Nations Championship in 1970 and 1973, and win it outright in 1971, 1975, 1976, 1978 and 1979. In that glorious decade Wales won the Grand Slam, beating all the other countries in the competition, three times, in 1971, 1976 and 1978. It produced such players as J P R Williams, Gerald Davies, Barry John and his successor Phil Bennett, Graham Price, Dave Morris and Mervyn Davies. The ground also saw one of the finest games of rugby ever played, the Barbarians v. New Zealand in 1973.

New Zealand has always had a special connection with Cardiff Arms Park over and above that of any other country, even including England. As the former captain of the All Blacks, Graham Mourie, who played in 1977–82, put it:

> Twickenham with those Rolls-Royces and bottles of champagne, Lansdowne Road and its terraces, Murrayfield and the Scottish Gloom, even Parc des Princes. All have their charms and quirks. But if you're an All Black and you're looking for rugby and especially a Test, then Cardiff Arms Park is the place.

Probably the most famous win in Wales' rugby history was gained against New Zealand there in December 1905, when the wing Teddy Morgan scored a try, giving Wales a 3–0 victory (in those days and for many years afterwards a try counted for 3 rather than 5 points). The New Zealanders claimed that one of their players, Deans, had also scored. In 1935 Wales won 13–12, with two tries by G R Rees-Jones and one by Claude Davey, and two conversions by Vivian Jenkins. In 1953 Wales won 13–8. The flanker Clem Thomas cross-kicked from a lineout and the centre Bleddyn Williams gathered the ball and passed it to the wing Ken Jones, who scored. The other flanker, Sid Judd, scored another try, and the wing Gwyn Rowlands kicked two conversions and one penalty.

Then came a succession of losses, of which the most controversial was by 12 points to 13 in 1978. Steve Fenwick kicked one penalty and Gareth Davies three, but the New Zealand forward Andy Haden was adjudged to have been knocked out of the lineout, so giving New Zealand a penalty that won the match. Some years later Haden admitted he had deliberately taken a dive! Yet before this lamented episode had taken place amid the modern splendours of the National Stadium, Wales had in half a century beaten New Zealand three times. In so doing it had – however odd it may seem – defined itself as a nation in the tin tabernacle that was the old Cardiff Arms Park.

Francis Chichester's round-the-world voyage
Peter Nichols

In 1966–7 a sixty-five-year-old Englishman, Francis Chichester, sailed alone around the world, stopping only once, in Australia.

A tall, thin, balding man with thick-lensed glasses, Chichester looked more like a prep school headmaster than an adventurer. He owned a small book and map shop in London. But the urge to subject himself to extreme tests had characterised his life. In his youth he had made a pioneering flight in a small aircraft from England to Australia.

In his mid fifties, Chichester developed lung cancer. The experience had a profound effect on him. He cured himself, largely by a vegetarian diet, and when he got better he took up sailing. In 1960, at the age of fifty-nine, he and four friends made a wager to race each other single-handedly in their four very different boats across the Atlantic. The course began at Plymouth's Eddystone lighthouse and finished at the Ambrose light vessel off New York harbour; the route between these two points was up to the racers. There were no other rules. Francis Chichester won the half-crown bet and the race.

Four years later, in 1964, a second race was held. Frenchman Eric Tabarly took the honours in twenty-seven days. Chichester came second – a new place for him and an ignominious position for a lone adventurer.

Single-handed racing hit the big time. A third OSTAR, as it came to be called (the *Observer* Single-handed Trans-Atlantic Race) was planned for 1968, but Chichester decided not to compete with the pack. He would be up against younger men sailing larger boats and the outcome must have been clear to him. He quietly set off to do something else.

Sailing alone around the world was nothing new. The Nova Scotian-born American Joshua Slocum, a sailing ship master beached in his middle years by the steam age, was the first to do it, in 1895–8. Eighteen men had circumnavigated the globe alone by the time Chichester set out in October 1966, but his voyage caught the public imagination as perhaps none other since Slocum's. It was no pleasure cruise. His route was down the Atlantic, east-about around the bottom of the world, back up the Atlantic. Virtually all the east-to-west part of his circumnavigation took place in a sea not found on most atlases but infamously known to all sailors as the Southern Ocean: the windswept southerly wastes of the Atlantic, Pacific, and Indian Oceans between latitudes 40 and 60 degrees south, between the habitable world and the Antarctic. This is an ocean where storm-force westerly winds develop and drive huge seas around the globe, unimpeded by land except at one fearsome place, Cape Horn, the scorpion tail tip of South America.

Chichester's circumnavigation was a savage intensification of the trials faced by a trans-Atlantic single-hander. His stated purpose was to beat the times of the old sailing ships; alone he would race them in a small modern yacht. It was a simple concept, dangerous and daring, and Chichester significantly upped the ante by his decision to stop only once, in Australia. Not only sailors, but the greater mass of the non-sailing public understood perfectly what was really going on here: it was an ordeal of the first magnitude. It was like climbing Everest alone.

For the British, whose stature on the world stage had been severely reduced since the Churchillian glory of World War Two, who had no plucky astronauts, whose government had recently been scandalised by an association between politicians and two prostitutes who had also been sharing their favours with the KGB, Chichester represented a longed-for but not forgotten ideal of heroic endeavour. Newspapers carried front page photos of the deeply-reefed *Gypsy Moth IV* battling gales off Cape Horn (taken by British warships and aircraft standing by, to Chichester's annoyance, to keep an eye on what had suddenly become a national interest). A quarter of a million people filled Plymouth Harbour when he arrived home on the evening of 28 May 1967 after more than seven months at sea. National television schedules were abandoned to cover the event live, and an entire nation watched hour after hour of *Gypsy Moth IV* sailing the last miles through a great fleet of ships and local boats that stretched from shore far out to sea, waiting through the long English twilight to see the lone sailor step ashore.

Later, in a ceremony consciously echoing the knighting of Sir Francis Drake by Queen Elizabeth I at Plymouth Hoe 400 years earlier, Chichester stepped ashore at Greenwich and knelt before Queen Elizabeth II, who dubbed him with a sword and granted him a knighthood. It was a masterstroke in a jaded era: every Briton knew the scene from school history books; here was legend made real on television and an intense *frisson* of national pride swept across the land.

Chichester's 226 days at sea did not better the clipper ships' record sailing times for the 28,500-mile voyage, but nobody cared. He was a national hero. His book of the voyage, *Gypsy Moth Circles the World*, published that same year, was an instant and lasting bestseller. His achievement had thrilled the public and resurrected glory for the island race.

He took to the Atlantic again in 1970 in a new boat, *Gypsy Moth V*, establishing a then record speed for a yacht of 1,000 miles sailed in five days. Struck with cancer once more in 1972, he attempted to cross the Atlantic again that year with the OSTAR fleet, but became too ill to continue. He was rescued at sea, against his will, by the intervention of the Royal Navy, which dropped his son Giles aboard *Gypsy Moth V*, and together they sailed back to Plymouth. Chichester died there on 17 August 1972.

Today, the 53-foot (16m) *Gypsy Moth IV* sits in a cement berth in Greenwich beside the great sailing clipper the *Cutty Sark*, an artefact of maritime history. But Chichester hated the boat in which he made his epochal voyage: 'Gypsy Moth IV has no sentimental value for me at all. She is cantankerous and difficult and needs a crew of three – a man to navigate, an elephant to move the tiller, and a 3'6" chimpanzee with arms 8' long to get about below and work some of the gear.' It didn't matter in the end. It simply proved the old saw: 'It's not the ships, but the men in them.'

Sir Francis Chichester bathing aboard Gyspy Moth V *during his solo transatlantic voyage, 1971*

Izaak Walton's Compleat Angler
Tom Fort

Poor old Walton! He wrote the immortal work with which his name will forever be linked for the best of reasons – to inform, to instruct, to divert – and sent it on its way with the gentlest and most modest of pushes: 'I shall stay [the reader] no longer than to wish him a rainy evening to read this following discourse: and that if he be an honest angler the east wind will never blow when he goes a-fishing.' The qualities and virtue of the man are transparent from the outset. Yet he has been much abused, most famously as 'the quaint, old, cruel coxcomb' by Byron, who wanted to put a hook in his gullet and have 'a small fish to pull it'.

But the charge which has come closest to sticking is that Walton did no more than help himself to other men's handiwork and pass it off as his own – that he was, in the mean-spirited words of the angling writer G E M Skues, 'a miserable old plagiarist who owed what he knew about fishing to a lady, Dame Juliana … and to that good, young gentleman, Charles Cotton'. The indictment is that, having nothing worthwhile to say on the subject himself, Walton merely embroidered the wisdom contained in the first of all fishing books in English, the *Treatyse of Fysshinge wyth an Angle* (attributed, wrongly, to the Abbess of St Albans, Dame Juliana Berners), and then appropriated the section on fly fishing for trout from his impressionable young friend Charles Cotton. It has been dusted off again in our times, by none other than that scourge of the political establishment Jeremy Paxman, for whom *The Compleat Angler* is 'virtually unreadable', its enduring success due to 'desperate relatives buying it as a present for the man they think has everything', its dialogue reading 'like a bad translation from Serbo-Croat'. With all due respect to Paxman, I fear that in his anxiety to denigrate Walton and extol the merits of 'a more important contributor to the history of fishing', Charles Cotton, he merely betrays his own prejudice in favour of fly fishing, which was Cotton's province (a fact openly conceded by Walton), rather than for the so-called coarse fishes – the savage pike, the stately carp, the portly chub, the toothsome eel – which were Old Izaak's passion.

This is not to deny the value of Cotton's contribution. That first, modest edition of *The Compleat Angler* contained nothing about fly fishing beyond a regurgitation of the basics laid down in the *Treatyse of Fysshinge*. As a consequence of its appearance, Walton – then already over sixty – and the much younger Cotton became friends. The elderly self-made man, pious and virtuous, and the dissolute, spendthrift young aristocrat formed an improbably close and affectionate bond. They talked, they exchanged letters and they fished together on Cotton's beloved Dove in Derbyshire, where he educated his spiritual father in the art of casting an artificial fly 'fine and far off' for the speckled trout. Cotton's

Izaak Walton in an illustration by Arthur Rackham from the 1931 Compleat Angler

twelve chapters – 'Instructions how to angle for a Trout or Grayling in a Clear Stream' – were ready (just) for the new edition, the fifth, published in 1676. With them, Walton's title was justified, and completeness was achieved.

From the angling point of view, Cotton was unarguably the original thinker of the two. But let no one doubt which was the master writer. Cotton follows Walton in casting his contribution in the form of dialogue. But in his amateurish hands, the lifeless exchanges between Piscator and Viator are no more than a means to arrive at his message, which is how to catch fish on a fly. For Walton, however, the message is in the conversation. He brings off something of a miracle by breathing life into this most restrictive and artificial of literary forms. Through it, he celebrates his deep love of England, its countryside, its people, its rivers, ponds and lakes, and its fish.

The form may be an obstacle for modern readers, and there are certainly dull and preachy passages. But the best policy is to stride past them, until you come to something like this: 'Doubt not therefore, sir, but that Angling is an Art, and an Art worthy of your learning: the question is rather whether you be capable of learning it.' A little later Walton is advising on the need for patience when using the grasshopper for chub: 'it is likely that the Chubs will sink down towards the bottom of the water at the first shadow of your rod, for a Chub is the fearfullest of fish.' This, to me, is irresistible. And *The Compleat Angler* is studded with such jewels. At his best, Walton speaks to us across the ages with amazing warmth and directness. Considering the sort of prose being written at the time (have you ever tried to wade through Milton's *Areopagitica?*) Walton's is marvellously simple. As J W Hills observed in his indispensable *History of Fly Fishing*, 'the charm of his style lies in the revelation which it gives of the man … shrewd and critical but also tolerant and wise … [N]o one has known better how to show what is best and deepest in his subject, even when dealing with what appears transitory or trivial.'

I cheerfully concede the flaws. Yes, he was a plagiarist – if being a plagiarist means taking someone else's work and transforming it into something much greater. He was credulous, occasionally wrong-headed, sometimes plain tedious. As a practical textbook *The Compleat Angler* is not far from being useless (although there is a vast amount of sound sense about the ways of fish). And, yes, it spawned a host of dreary imitations.

Who cares? Is it a crime that he should have retrieved other men's ideas and learning from what would otherwise have been irredeemable obscurity? Does it matter that his advice on catching a pike with a live frog would today land you in court on a cruelty charge? That he talked utter nonsense about the birth of eels and much else? It matters nothing. Lesser men who knew much more about how to catch fish have come and gone, and Walton endures. The fact that an edition of *The Compleat Angler* has appeared for every one of the 350 or so years since its first publication is one sign of the hold it has exercised, not just in the United Kingdom but across the civilised world. It is one of those books – like *Pilgrim's Progress* – that just about everyone has heard of. But it is something more too, something far more precious and vital than a mere monument, a milestone. It is a book worth reading, for itself.

Henry Cooper's 1963 fight with Cassius Clay
Reg Gutteridge

It must be the most photographed punch in boxing history – a left hook delivered with power and perfect timing to floor a then bragging upstart, Cassius Marcellus Clay, in a ring pitched on the hallowed turf of Wembley Stadium on the damp, overcast night of 18 June 1963.

The crowd had paid 12/6d (62½p) to stand or six guineas (£6.30p) to share a ringside view with Elizabeth Taylor and Richard Burton. The nation cheered for a Cooper victory. Henry Cooper was more a gentleman-at-arms than a professional pugilist. The fight was not a world heavyweight title – the awesome American Sonny Liston held the undisputed crown. Cooper had been chosen as a proposed work-out for Clay's already planned challenge match with Liston.

But Clay's all-white millionaire management syndicate from Kentucky had seriously underrated the admired British heavyweight champion. Cooper was to come within seconds of greatness in the non-title fight. He buttoned the tabloid-tagged 'Louisville Lip'.

Clay entered the ring wearing a pantomime crown he had spotted in the wings offstage at the London Palladium, which promoter Jack Solomon, who rivalled Barnum for showmanship, had hired for the pre-fight weigh-in. A huge crowd had thronged the West End at midday to catch sight of the handsome, brash Clay, who had predicted Cooper 'would fall in five'. Cooper, meanwhile, used his identical twin brother George as a decoy to avoid any overzealous backslapping and handshaking outside the Palladium. At the weigh-in itself Cooper scaled only thirteen stone three and a quarter pounds. Clay, who had won an Olympic Gold Medal at light-heavyweight three years earlier, had since muscled to fourteen stone eleven pounds. Cooper's wily veteran manager, Jim Wicks, later admitted he had put metal insoles in Cooper's boxing boots, intending to lessen Clay's weight advantage. But the ploy was wasted. Clay was not a man to be fazed.

''Enry's 'Ammer' – that devastating left hand – was the best weapon in Cooper's armoury. He began with the typical English-style left, a range-tester as reliable as the Greenwich time-signal. Clay, who had won his eighteen paid fights and never taken a count, had been reared with the gift of jab and gab, but Cooper was not afraid of him. The angle of Clay's blows was cutting rather than punishing. During the second round, however, Cooper's scar tissue began to bleed.

In the third round, a sharp photographer caught a tuft of horsehair floating below the ring lights: Clay's left glove had torn at the seam of the stitched thumb. (Gloves then were padded with horsehair; now they are made with attached thumbs and no stitching in order to prevent movement.) I was sitting alongside the chief inspector of the Boxing

Overleaf: 'Enry's 'Ammer: Henry Cooper moves in on Cassius Clay, 18 June 1963

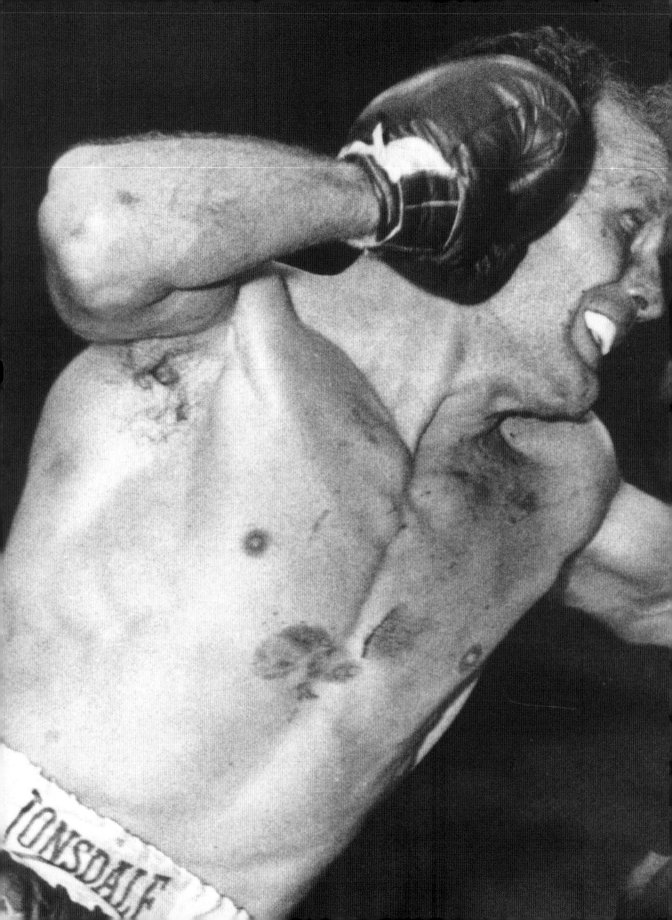

Board of Control. This being the days before spare gloves had to be kept available under the ring, he immediately trotted across the pitch to the dressing rooms to find a replacement.

In the fourth, Cooper backed Clay onto the ropes. I was close enough on the ring apron to have touched Clay's feet. Cooper switched his left lead to an arc hook – considered the most difficult blow to block – which landed plumb on Clay's jaw.

Clay sagged on bent knees, his eyes in orbit. But he instinctively pulled himself up as referee Tommy Little, a London ex-boxer turned newsagent, began a count. He rose as the bell ended the round and was able to head for his corner.

The crowd were still roaring when he sank onto the stool. Worried trainer Angelo Dundee doused him with water and smartly made play to the referee of the split glove, which was already open at the thumb. Dundee had no need to worsen the split, but doesn't mind being given credit for anxiously complaining that his man shouldn't have to continue. But the glove (later displayed at a Soho betting shop) was never changed.

Dick Reekie, Dundee's faithful assistant second, later confirmed to me that the confusion and concern in Clay's corner had the referee urging the seconds to be prepared for the timekeeper's call of 'Seconds Out' and be ready to get Clay out for the fifth. How long Clay actually rested between rounds has been a matter of controversy ever since, with some claiming that a whole extra minute was added to the scheduled minute's rest. Cooper himself naturally believed the overtime was lengthy. If only the famous punch had landed earlier…

Clay's powers of recovery, subsequently shown against Frazier and Foreman, were remarkable. The head man of his Kentucky syndicate was yelling 'Be serious!' when action resumed. But Clay was not acting. His fifth-round boxing was clinical, with barely a blow missed. Cooper's eyebrow cascaded blood until he was mercifully rescued by referee Little only a minute into the round. He left the ring unbowed. Clay, to his credit, refused to wear his stage crown out of the ring.

Was Cooper robbed of glory? We shall never know. Surprisingly, the overnight newspaper reports made little play of a delay. The only acceptable evidence is the recording of the live BBC radio broadcast. There, bell-end to restart of the fourth and fifth rounds are stopwatch-timed at 66 seconds.

The return match with Clay (by now Muhammad Ali) put his world title at stake. It took place at the Arsenal Football Club ground in London in 1966. The gate receipts were higher than for the England World Cup-winning final at Wembley the same year. Cooper was never off his feet and neither was Ali. The points were close when Cooper was again cut up. He was beaten in six rounds.

Cooper and Ali have continued to meet socially with sincere mutual respect. Cooper won three heavyweight Lonsdale Belts and was knighted. Ali was rightly voted Sportsman of the Century. I count myself honoured to have known them.

The FA Cup final
Brian Glanville

Beyond all doubt, the Football Association Cup is the mother of all football competitions. Initiated in 1872, it was the first of its kind, and its very success led to the foundation of the Football League – this because the professional clubs which had sprung up in England during the 1880s needed, economically, something beyond a tournament of sudden death elimination in which they would play at most a handful of matches or perhaps even as few as one.

The FA Cup final, which began quietly enough – albeit at a famous location, the Oval Cricket Ground in Kennington, South London, venue for cricket's Test matches and the games of the Surrey club – took little time to become massively popular. By 1892 it had outgrown the Oval and moved north to Fallowfield and Everton. In 1895 it returned to South London, to the old Crystal Palace – that is to say, the area where the Crystal Palace itself, that huge attraction of the Great Exhibition of 1851, was moved from Kensington – where crowds grew exponentially till they were far in excess of 100,000.

From 1923 till 2000, the final was indelibly associated with Wembley Stadium, the first venue of its kind, where some 200,000 fans famously attended the 1923 final. Now, while we await the belated reconstruction of Wembley, the final has moved to the ultra-modern Millennium Stadium at Cardiff, with its retractable roof. Two thousand and one saw a dramatic baptism, when Liverpool's late surge snatched the FA Cup from Arsenal.

Who, to be fair, were somewhat used to having it snatched from them in the past. In 1927, at Wembley, there was the final when the Cup went out of England for the one and only time; to Cardiff, in fact, Cardiff City beating the Gunners on the strangest and most bathetic of goals. Danny Lewis, a Welshman in the Arsenal goal, moved to deal with an unthreatening shot, only for the ball to spin out of his hands, roll off his crisp new shiny jersey and cross the line. It's said that ever since, when they've played in the final, Arsenal have carefully had the keeper's jersey washed beforehand.

Five years later, again at Wembley, Arsenal were stricken with the so-called Over the Line goal, when Newcastle United's Richardson, chasing a long ball down the right, pulled it across goal after, as was shown on photos and newsreels, it had crossed the goal line. The Gunners' defence stopped, and Allen headed in. The goal was given; Newcastle United won 2–1. They beat Arsenal again in the 1952 final when the Gunners' right-back, Walley Barnes, caught his studs in the turf, twisted his knee and had to go off the field. No substitution then; Arsenal had to continue with ten men. As would Manchester City in 1955 against Newcastle (right-back Jimmy Meadows the victim), Manchester United in 1957 against Aston Villa (goalkeeper Ray Wood) and Nottingham Forest in

Overleaf: *West Bromwich Albion celebrate victory against Birmingham City, April 1931*

1959, though they beat Luton (broken leg for Roy Dwight, cousin of Elton John), not to mention Blackburn v. Wolves in 1960 and Leicester City v. Spurs in 1961.

In 2001 there was a furore when Manchester United, then the Cup holders, withdrew from the competition to take part in a half-baked so-called Club World Cup competition in Brazil. For this United themselves were most unfairly blamed, the truth being that they came under intolerable pressure to go from government and the FA themselves, since it was mistakenly feared that not to do so would harm England's doomed attempt to stage the 2006 World Cup.

The FA Cup was based initially on the so-called Cock House Cup at Harrow School, the alma mater of C W Alcock, who became secretary of the Football Association in 1870. Among the original fifteen teams who competed were the famous Scottish amateurs, Queen's Park, who actually got all the way to the semi-finals without playing a game! This was because they had either byes or walkovers and, having drawn the first semi-final against the public schoolboys of the Wanderers, were obliged to withdraw because they couldn't repeat the journey to London. The following year they were exempt till the semi-finals, as a gesture to their travelling difficulties, but were obliged to scratch again, this time against Oxford University. Wanderers on this occasion only were exempt as holders till the final, which they won; as indeed they did against the Royal Engineers in 1874. This third success meant the Cup was theirs in perpetuity, but they generously restored it to the FA. They would win it again in 1876 (a 3–0 replay against Old Etonians), 1877 and 1878.

Their salient player, himself an Old Etonian, was the red-bearded Honourable (later Lord) A F Kinnaird, a formidable competitor. Once when his wife told one of his friends she was afraid he might one day come home with a broken leg, the reply was 'Don't worry; if he does, it won't be his own'. In later years, Lord Kinnaird became chairman of the Football Association. C W Alcock himself was a Wanderers captain.

How things have changed! On the occasion of the second final, at the Oval, attendance 3,000, kick-off was at 11.00 a.m. (actually delayed half an hour) so that the contestants could watch the Boat Race. Chivalry in those early amateur days was *de rigueur*. In the replayed 1875 final between Old Etonians and the Royal Engineers, C J Ottaway, a superb all-round athlete, had to come off the field with a bad ankle injury, leaving the Etonians a man short. Presented with a crisis of conscience, Major Marindin of the Royal Engineers, himself an Old Etonian, voluntarily left the field.

Professionalism crept in in the 1880s, though it wasn't legitimised till 1886. This was when the invasion of London by northern fans 'oop for the Coop' became established, the *Pall Mall Gazette* describing Blackburn supporters as 'a strange and uncouth horde'. No fewer than four times did Blackburn Rovers reach the final between 1882 and 1886, winning three in a row between 1884 and 1886. Blackburn Olympic, though short-lived, were the first pro team to win the final, against the Old Etonians after extra time in 1883.

Attendances were now rising fast. In 1895 42,560 saw the first final to be held at the Crystal Palace, a Midlands derby in which Aston Villa beat West Bromwich Albion. The

first 100,000-plus crowd came a decade later, in 1905, Villa beating Newcastle United. When Villa won it again in 1913, it was in front of 120,081. In 1920, 1921 and 1922, Chelsea's Stamford Bridge was the scene of the final. Then to Wembley.

And an infinity of memories. The so-called Matthews Cup Final of 1953, for example, seen as a last chance for the incomparable right-winger Stanley Matthews of Blackpool to gain a winners' medal, after finishing on the losing side in 1948 and 1951. This he breathlessly did, against a Bolton side reduced to nine fit men who gallantly resisted till Matthews, wriggling and dribbling his way to the by-line, crossed for Perry to score the clinching goal.

Or in later years the amazing save by Jim Montgomery of Sunderland, turning Peter Lorimer of Leeds' point-blank shot onto the crossbar, enabling his Second Division team to beat the favourites. That was in 1973. Three years later another Second Division team, Southampton, with a single goal by Stokes, had the temerity to beat mighty Manchester United.

Always dramatic, never predictable, its final the occasion for some of the most memorable moments in the history of British football, the FA Cup will surely never lose its allure.

The sons of two Spurs players hold the cup in the Tottenham tour of triumph, May 1962

The Derby
Robin Oakley

For owners, trainers and jockeys there is no race quite like the one-and-a-half mile Epsom Derby, the Blue Riband of the Turf and a supreme test of both horse and rider over its unique switchback course. Success in other races, like the Prix de L'Arc de Triomphe or newer events in the Middle East and Japan, may be deeply coveted and carry bigger prize money, but the Epsom Derby is the one they all want to win.

When American John Galbreath declared in 1972 'Anyone who doesn't consider the Epsom Derby one of the greatest sporting events in the world must be out of his mind', he may have been a little prejudiced: his colt Roberto had just won the contest. But the famed Italian breeder Federico Tesio was no less of an enthusiast. He claimed: 'The Thoroughbred exists because its selection has depended not on experts, technicians or zoologists, but on a piece of wood: the winning post of the Epsom Derby.' No other race has the history and prestige of the Derby and no other course provides such a test of the three-year-old Thoroughbred as the annual 'scurry over Surrey' in the first week in June.

To win the Derby you have to be something special. No horse without speed can do it. But you need stamina too and the character to cope not just with the remarkable terrain, but with the jangle of the fairground and a big day buzz like no other from the 100,000-plus crowd. Everybody who is anybody, from the Queen downwards, is there on Derby Day as a field of around fifteen Thoroughbreds, trained to the minute, their nerves jangling, sets off from a low point on the Epsom Downs on the far side of the funfair which occupies the centre of the course. Many of those watching will bear memories of the great horses they have seen swoop to victory in the past, legends like Sea Bird II, Nijinsky or Mill Reef.

First the horses climb uphill for four furlongs, streaming round a gradual right-hand bend. Then comes their only chance to settle as they switch left to the inner rail and head up to the top of Tattenham Hill. There follows a pell-mell dash down the slope to the sharp left-hand bend round Tattenham Corner.

Lester Piggott, winner of an unparalleled nine Derbies, says of the potential Derby winner: 'Size is less important than the manner of racing. You need a horse that can lay up handy, a few places behind the leaders: getting too far back at Epsom can be disastrous as there is no part of the course where you can readily make up ground forfeited early on. You have to get up into a reasonable place and keep out of trouble as beaten horses fall back on the downhill run.'

Even when Tattenham Corner has been negotiated, the horses face a further test in front of the stands. The finishing straight is nearly four furlongs long, and as they reach the final 200 yards tired three-year-olds running through a wall of noise confront not just a further gut-busting rise to the finishing post, but a camber which tilts them in towards the inside rail, making it hard for their riders to keep them on a true course to the line.

The Derby is the leading feature of the five English Classics for three-year-olds (the rest being the 1,000 Guineas and the Oaks, both restricted to fillies, and the 2,000 Guineas and St Leger, the other two races forming the Triple Crown for colts). The race has founded and broken the fortunes of great families, it has created folk heroes of horses and men and it has in its time been Britain's greatest picnic day out. In the nineteenth century even Parliament used to be adjourned for three days to accommodate the Epsom meeting.

Perhaps the most sensational Derby ever was in 1913 when the suffragette Emily Davison threw herself in front of the King's horse Anmer as the field rounded Tattenham Corner, later dying from her injuries. Then the favourite Craganour, having passed the post first, was disqualified for interference and the 100–1 outsider Aboyeur was awarded the race. (The only other Derby winner to be disqualified was the 1844 victor Running Rein, who was discovered to be a four-year-old.)

Horses whose names will forever be associated with Epsom's great race include the ill-fated Shergar, later kidnapped and killed, whose winning margin of ten lengths in 1981 remains a record. Lammtarra, the 1995 winner, clocked the record time for the race, which he completed in 2 minutes 32.31 seconds, beating the record previously held by Mahmoud, hand-timed at 2 minutes 33.8 seconds in 1936. Lammtarra, who only ran in three other races, retired from racing unbeaten. So did Bahram, whose nine successes included the Triple Crown. Amato, who won in 1838, had never raced before the Derby and never raced after it. Although colts cannot run in the Oaks, fillies may run in the Derby. The last one to do so and win was Fifinella in 1916, when the race was run at Newmarket. Two days later she took the Oaks as well.

Among jockeys Lester Piggott reigns supreme. He scored the first of his nine Derby wins on Never Say Die in 1954 when he was only eighteen and his last on Teenoso in 1983. Fred Archer rode five, driving Bend Or home in 1880 solely with his legs. He had dropped his whip because his arm was too weakened from being savaged by a horse.

The charmer Steve Donoghue rode six Derby winners, perhaps the most remarkable success among them being the 1921 victory on Humorist, a horse who had a rogue's reputation after losing several races by faltering in the last hundred yards. Donoghue forfeited his retainer with Lord Derby to ride the horse at Epsom and won by a neck without using the whip, saying 'I would rather have cut off my right hand than even show him the whip'. A few weeks later Humorist was being prepared for Ascot when he died in his box from a massive haemorrhage. It turned out that all his life he had suffered chronic consumption and his one remaining lung had finally given way.

Sometimes victory in the Derby proves elusive for the very best. The great Sir Gordon Richards, the most prolific rider of winners in Britain, only won the Derby on Pinza at his twenty-eighth and final attempt in the Coronation year of 1953.

Overleaf: *The Blue Riband of the turf:* The Finish of the Epsom Derby in 1822 *by John Sinclair*

The most successful Derby trainers all date from an age when the competition was perhaps a little less intense. Robert Robson, Fred Darling and John Porter each won the race seven times. Among owners, the present Aga Khan deserves a special mention. Although he has yet to match his grandfather's record of five winners in the race, when Sinndar won for him in the year 2000 it was the fourth time he had won with a horse he had bred himself.

The Derby has inevitably been the subject of some spectacular gambles over the years. In 1967 William Hill laid American owner Raymond Guest £50,000 to £500 and £12,500 to £500 the place against his unraced two-year-old colt winning the Derby the next year; when Sir Ivor won the 1968 race he started at 5–4 on. Hermit's victory in 1867 famously ruined the Marquis of Hastings. Hastings was a high-stakes gambler who had eloped with Lady Florence Paget when she slipped out of the back of Swan and Edgar's on a shopping expedition with her fiancé Henry Chaplin. When he heard that the high-class Hermit had broken a blood vessel in his final gallop, Hastings laid against him for huge sums. Somehow Captain James Machell, Hermit's trainer, managed to patch him up and he won in one late lunge by a neck. Hastings lost at least £100,000 on the race, a fair amount of it to Chaplin, but was the first to go up and pat Hermit's neck. He died in penury the next year aged only twenty-six, whispering on his deathbed: 'Hermit fair broke my heart, but I didn't show it, did I?'

Perhaps the most famous Derby gamble, though, was the very first one. In the garden of The Oaks in 1774, after they had jointly had the idea of founding the race, the then Lord Derby and his friend Sir Charles Bunbury, senior steward of the Jockey Club, tossed a coin to see whom the race should be named after. Had it gone the other way Britain's best three-year-olds would have been racing for the last 220 years in the Bunbury.

Five O'Clock Sports Report
Frank Keating

They turned down Sloane Street and the warm windows cast light patches on the pavement between the
blobs of the street lamps. The same tune muffled through the walls as they passed from house to house,
fading then swelling between the space of each lighted window. 'Hey up, Dad, that's Sports Report,
I'll race you...'

from The Blinder by Barry Hines

It was already past four o'clock on the afternoon of the first Saturday of the year of 1948.
League football matches all over the country were finishing. At Twickenham, England's
rugby union international against Australia had already ended. In studio 4A at BBC
radio's Broadcasting House in central London, the fraught producer had still not decided
upon the introductory theme music for a debutant programme due to take the air live at
5.30 that very evening. He answered a telephone call from the BBC gramophone library
two floors down. Would he have time to listen to a final batch of possibilities? He
bounded down the staircase two at a time.

Years later, Angus Mackay recalled: 'For weeks, my assistant Hugh Driver and I had
wearily listened to countless dozens of tunes. Not one melody remotely hit the precise
note. Till that call almost an hour before 'on air' – when the first one we heard was
Out of the Blue, composed by Hubert Bath. "Eureka!" I grabbed the disc from the
turntable and careered back up the stairs with it.'

Deedum – deedum – deedum – deedum – dee-diddly-dum-deedaah! Mr Bath's catchy march,
bristling with urgency and anticipated delights, has ever since pluperfectly topped and
tailed BBC radio's winter Saturday national institution called *Sports Report* – never missing
a beat since that first transmission on 3 January 1948 and now well into its second half-
century and sailing inexorably and serenely on to its next. As an uninterrupted
broadcasting long-runner *Sports Report*'s venerability is unique, unmatched even by such
BBC stalwarts as *Letter from America* (first heard in 1950) and *The Archers* (1951). *Sports Report*
is a social and cultural British totem: it was first heard that January evening only two days
after the British railways were nationalised; it is older than the National Health Service
(founded in July that year), older than Prince Charles (born November 1948). *Out of the*
Blue burst with gaiety into the consciousness of the nation that January to invigorate an
austere, grey, Cold-War-weary Britain, in which bread and bacon, milk and meat, were
still severely rationed. So was petrol; even if you could afford a new Austin A40 family
saloon at £315, you were restricted to no more than ninety miles a month. Beer cost
1s 4d a pint (7p), the same as a packet of ten cigarettes. For recreation and entertainment,
there was the cinema; through 1948 Britain's *Kind Hearts and Coronets* was vying to attract
even more queues around the picture houses than Hollywood's Oscar-laden *Treasure of the*

Sierra Madre. But by far the most immense queues were those formed in the mass by those desperate to seek the relief – and the release – of spectator sport.

In that 1947–8 football season, English League football attendances shattered all records, soaring past an astonishing 40 million. (In Scotland, 153,570 attended a midweek afternoon match in Glasgow.) Bombed-out Old Trafford meant Manchester United still had to share their City neighbour's ground at Maine Road – where a still unsurpassed 83,260 squashed in to see United draw 1–1 with Arsenal two Saturdays after *Sports Report*'s first mellifluous announcement of itself. So *deedum – deedum – deedum – deedum – dee-diddly-dum-deedaah!* was a perfectly timed overture and call to attention. Not that Mackay's commission had itself come 'out of the blue'. The previous October, the former Edinburgh news journalist, who had first joined the Corporation in 1936, received a memo from 'Assistant to Light Programme Controller' enquiring whether he would 'care to consider trying his hand at putting a sports programme on the air at 5.30 on Saturdays?' Care to consider? Try his hand? Mackay leapt at it. The now legendary Scot was to remain *Sports Report*'s onlie begetter and inspiration for almost a quarter of a century till his retirement in 1972, and his spirit still haunts the spellbinding ether which emanates around Britain and, now, far beyond every Saturday teatime of every winter. Wherever I am, whatever I'm doing, when *Out of the Blue* summons the faithful to their pontifical high mass each week, I think with fond gratitude of maestro Mackay. Of course, no recording was made of that historic preface to immortal radio fame, but the dog-eared, treasured script has survived – the very one read by that fruity-voiced 'steam radio' familiar with the Winco-moustache, Raymond Glendenning, as soon as Mackay himself had manually faded down his newfound melody on the studio gramophone:

> Hello there, sports fans, and welcome to *Sports Report*, a weekly programme of the air with a roving microphone to bring you not only the football results but up-to-the-minute accounts from all parts of the country, and an 'open' microphone over which we shall be airing the personal views of experts on topics of the moment... But first, this afternoon's classified football results...

No historian can be sure who actually read *Sports Report*'s first tabulation of results. Some say the smoked-salmon smoothness of actor-announcer John Webster's voice was not heard till a few Saturdays later, and that the elocuted precision of presenter Robin Boyle provided the debutant programme's opening Solemn Introit. Certainly, Webster was to set the standard in gravity – and maintain it for years – after which James Alexander Gordon's dulcets became a weekly elucidation of utter grandeur to the end of the century and beyond. As the writer P J Kavanagh put it: 'Gordon makes the reading of football results each week sound like a highly original found-poem.' Exactly. 'Plymouth Argyle one, Exeter City nil'... poet *and* (to some) tragedian. Or as Jeremy Clarke asked in the

A father and son listen to the sports results on the wireless, late 1940s

Sunday Telegraph: 'Has anyone ever gathered in that great Victorian railway terminus of the nation's consciousness known as *Sports Report* and heard this marvellous man say "Heart of Midlothian nil, Hamilton Academical one" without feeling that the world isn't such a bad place after all?'

Sports Report's first ever match report, in fact, concerned rugby union – England's game at Twickenham that January afternoon finishing in time for reporter Frank Shaw to drive to Broadcasting House and be first on, breathlessly scripted, with Australia's 11–0 victory ('A K Walker's thrilling try … took him almost the length of the left touchline'). Then Glendenning introduced the first ever 'live' soccer account transmitted on *Sports Report* – in the rich brown-windsor Wessex tones of BBC poetry producer and to-be-legendary cricket commentator John Arlott. Arlott had watched Portsmouth play Huddersfield Town at Fratton Park before taking the local train three stops where, by Mackay's arrangement, he unlocked the door of the unmanned, emergency 'studio' cupboard in the basement of the Portsmouth Civic Offices, clamped on earphones and, in solitary expectation, waited for Mackay's cue before telling an enthralled nation: 'This game was a magnificent one to watch because the forward lines of both Portsmouth and Huddersfield kept up on the attack, with the wing-halves of each side bringing the ball to them along the ground…'

From the BBC Manchester studios Alan Clarke then told of City's Maine Road match against Aston Villa before, back in London, Glendenning first interviewed celebrated Fleet Streeter Peter Wilson – who had sailed back across the Atlantic over Christmas from seeing the Joe Louis v. 'Jersey' Joe Walcott heavyweight boxing match fully a month before – then debated with another leading sportswriter, Alan Hoby, the radical proposition that Britain's athletes should be given a part-time government 'wage' to train for the upcoming 1948 summer Olympic Games in London. Then Mackay himself slapped *Out of the Blue* on the turntable, the studio presenter announced that *Jazz Club* would follow the *Six-o'Clock News*, and Mackay took Driver, Glendenning, Wilson, Hoby and his secretary Miss Reeves across Langham Place to the BBC Club and, as any good Scot should, ordered whisky chasers with their pints.

As they toasted themselves in first-night relief, as performers do, can any of them have realised what they had begun that midwinter afternoon? Or the household radio figures who would follow them? Eamonn Andrews was soon to take over from Glendenning, and was followed as presenter, after fourteen years of paramount mould-establishing distinction, by such as Robin Marlar, Des Lynam, Peter Jones, John Inverdale, Ian Payne, and Mark Pougatch. Skilful, talented broadcasters, and fond, famed, familiar voices from 'out of the blue'…

Deedum – deedum – deedum – deedum – dee-diddly-dum-deedaah!

On Saturdays, at teatime in the winters – every single teatime, every single winter – the mystical Age of Steam lives on.

The Five/Six Nations
J P R Williams

I have lived with the Five Nations Rugby Tournament since I was a young boy. For me, it was always the highlight of the first three months of the year.

There have been many changes to the tournament in that time. From 1949 until 1973 the Five Nations spread itself from January through to April with one match per weekend. Following increasing commercial pressures, double-header matches – i.e. two matches each weekend – were introduced in 1974, followed more recently by triple-headers, with the abandonment of the traditional January start. It is interesting, incidentally, that of the five nations taking part, only Wales, England, Scotland and Ireland were members of the International Rugby Board until the 1970s, though the fifth nation, France, had taken part in the tournament for many years prior to this. The Five Nations became the Six Nations with the inclusion of Italy in 2000, and the 2002 season's competition finished with England playing Italy in Rome on 7 April. There will be even more changes in 2003, the decision having been taken to condense the tournament into seven weekends, starting later and finishing earlier.

I was fortunate enough to play in the Five Nations for twelve years, spanning three decades from 1969 to 1981. My first involvement in the tournament was my first cap in the Wales v. Scotland match at Murrayfield in 1969. I could not believe the number of Welsh people in Edinburgh that Saturday morning. A walk down Princes Street was just like being back in Cardiff on the day of a home international. There seemed to have been a mass exodus from Wales and many people were bumping into friends and acquaintances and asking 'What are you doing up here, Dai? Up for the match, are you?' It was already obvious to me on that first occasion that supporters had saved up for the previous two years to have their trip to Murrayfield. It brought home to me the fact that the Five Nations is not just a rugby tournament, but one big social gathering. Supporters have their favourite trips, whether it be away to Murrayfield, Lansdowne Road, Twickenham or, at that time, Stades Colombes. (The French stadium moved to Parc des Princes in 1973 and subsequently to Stade de France, which has not been a lucky ground so far for the French.)

The Five Nations has always been the top competition in the northern hemisphere, and in the tremendous Welsh sides I was privileged to be part of in the 1970s we never got fed up with being successful or became complacent, regardless of who we were playing. The interesting thing about the tournament is that in spite of England's recent superiority each game is a one-off. This puts pressure on coaches, in that it is difficult to build for the future with the supporters of each country demanding success in the next game, whichever it may be. There have been many surprise results over the years, as exemplified by England's failure to win the Grand Slam at the final hurdle over the three seasons to 2001. Wales were the victors at Wembley in 1999, Scotland at Murrayfield in 2000 and Ireland at Lansdowne Road in 2001. It can be difficult for the surprise winners too, of course, as they then have to live up to their new-found status by playing in the next match, where it is not unusual for them to come unstuck. The Six Nations is a great leveller.

The Grand Slam – winning every game of the tournament – is the highest achievement for an international team in the northern hemisphere, an incredibly difficult feat however strong the side. In my time it meant winning four consecutive matches – which I was lucky enough to achieve on three occasions with Wales, in 1971, 1976 and 1978 – whereas nowadays it means winning five consecutive matches.

Cardiff Arms Park in the old days was something of a fortress for the Welsh side, who defended themselves there against all comers, particularly in the 1970s. In fact, I did not lose a Five Nations game at Cardiff during my whole career! As for the away trips, every one was different in its own way: the mass of red in Princes Street for the Murrayfield game; the crowds of Guinness-drinkers in the Dublin pubs for the Irish game at Lansdowne Road, with its unique railway line running just behind the posts; the austere atmosphere of HQ, Twickenham. Twickenham was my most successful ground, though the playing surface was not particularly good and the grass was always kept on the long side. Being a medical student and doctor in London during my time playing for Wales, I was even more determined to beat England, as most of my friends were English and it became a personal vendetta. Perhaps this had something to do with my having scored four tries at HQ!

I always particularly enjoyed my trips to France, which were totally different from the trips to Scotland, Ireland or England. My first game in France was at Stades Colombes, later the venue for the filming of *Chariots of Fire*. The atmosphere at the stadium was always very noisy, with several bands apparently playing in the crowd at once. Interestingly, at that time these were almost away games for the French team too, since most of the players came from the South of France and the Paris stadium was a long way from their homes. Nowadays, however, since the formation of Stade de France, many of the French players are based in Paris.

Most of my fondest memories of the Five Nations are of games against France, one of the toughest of which was in 1971 when we managed to come out winners by nine points to five in the last game at Stades Colombes. This was an important precursor to the ground-breaking British Lions tour of New Zealand in 1971, in which there were fourteen Welsh players in the side. Indeed, I believe that this match at Stades Colombes, in which we defended for long periods of the game, was crucial in bolstering the players' belief that they could succeed against the odds in New Zealand, as we proceeded to do, becoming in the process the first British Lions side ever to win a Test series there – a rugby triumph that might never have happened without the Five Nations.

J P R Williams in action in 1978

Roger Bannister's four-minute mile
Terry O'Connor

In many ways, the story behind the legendary first sub-four-minute mile, achieved by Roger Bannister at Oxford on 6 May 1954, is even more intriguing than the race itself – a historic event I was privileged to witness in person. Behind Bannister, a complex character and a reluctant runner averse to media attention, this amazing saga boasted a cast of many players.

Speculation about an athlete running the mile in under four minutes first surfaced seriously in 1923 when that greatest of all Olympic athletes, the Finn Paavo Nurmi, added a 4 minute 10.4 second mile to his other remarkable achievements. Jack Lovelock (New Zealand), Glen Cunningham (USA) and Britain's versatile Sydney Wooderson helped take the time down to 4 minutes 6.4 seconds. Then during the Second World War two Swedish runners, Arne Andersson and Gundar Haegg, managed to make the front pages of Britain's newspapers as they broke the mile record five times, leaving Haegg in command on 4 minutes 1.4 seconds in 1945.

It was not until after the 1952 Olympic Games in Helsinki that speculation about the four-minute barrier emerged again in Britain. This was due to the arrival on the track at Oxford University of a young medical student called Roger Bannister.

Bannister was one of the favourites to win the metric mile after running a time of 2 minutes 51 seconds in a secret three-quarter-mile trial before he left London for Helsinki. But while he undoubtedly had talent, he lacked experience, especially of running against fiercely contested international fields. He was also so under-trained for the Olympic battles ahead that he became obsessed with conserving energy at all costs. Little wonder, then, that he finished fourth behind Josef Barthel from tiny Luxembourg.

If the British champion had won at Helsinki it might have proved the end of his athletic career. As it was, after pressure from friends and from his own nagging ambition, Bannister decided on continuing for two more years. In private he nursed the hope of becoming the first man to break four minutes for the mile. Although in his book *First Four Minutes* he wrote 'Records should be the servants, not the master of the athlete, preparing him for forthcoming encounters', Bannister was astute enough to realise that he dreamed of a record which would always be remembered.

In December 1952 Bannister heard the news that John Landy, an Australian runner who had failed to reach the Olympic 1,500 meters final, had run the mile in 4 minutes 2.1 seconds, followed by 4 minutes 2.6 seconds. Coached by an eccentric former marathon runner, Percy Cerutty, Landy did not suffer from the training inhibitions which haunted his British rival; he just increased his mileage and ran fast up and down the sand

3 minutes 59.4 seconds: Bannister achieves the first ever sub-four-minute mile, Iffley, Oxford, 6 May 1954

dunes. Fearing that Landy would visit Europe to find better opposition, Bannister decided to make a record attempt at Oxford in April 1953, with Olympian Chris Chataway helping to set the pace. But although Bannister broke Sydney Wooderson's British record with 4 minutes 3.6 seconds, he was still nearly thirty yards short of his target.

It was now obvious that Bannister was not yet physically or mentally ready for the mighty challenge. During the winter of 1953–4 he increased his training schedules alongside Chataway and Chris Brasher. Fortunately also in attendance during most sessions was the enlightened Austrian-born coach Franz Stampfl, who, while never afforded the recognition he deserved by Bannister himself, was to become a major influence on British athletics. Following his Corinthian principles, Bannister wanted to do everything on his own, but Stampfl nonetheless continued to give him invaluable advice, arguing that anyone who could run three laps in around 2 minutes 50 seconds could achieve the Everest target. Although there was never any question of Bannister emulating Landy's twenty-mile daily runs, the medical student was better prepared for the 1954 season.

The venue for that year's May attempt was again to be the miler's favourite cinder track, Iffley Road in Oxford. Apart from Cambridge University man Brasher, later to win the 3,000-metres steeplechase at the 1956 Melbourne Olympics, it was altogether an Oxford affair. In the background were two former dark blue sprinters, the McWhirter twins Norris and Ross, who planned for the event as meticulously as might be expected from the original authors of the *Guinness Book of Records*.

When the day arrived the weather was just as Bannister had feared – lashing rain and a blustery wind. After visiting his hospital, St Mary's, he caught a train from Paddington to Oxford. Stampfl joined him (though not by arrangement). The coach quickly realised the fears haunting his pupil: 'You have reached your peak physically and psychologically,' Stampfl told him, 'so forget the weather. You can run a time of 3 minutes 56.7 seconds, which is sufficient to counter any wind.'

Even during the warm-up at the nearby rugby ground there was still talk of postponing the attempt, but Brasher said 'Let us give it a go'. As the six competitors lined up at 6.00 p.m., the flag of St George hung limp from a nearby church; the wind had at last abated.

As planned, Brasher went into the lead, Bannister following in search of a dream which had tantalised runners for more than thirty years. Midway through the first lap, full of confidence and surging with energy, Bannister called on Brasher to increase the pace. This was ignored – wisely, as the time of 57 seconds at 440 yards proved. A hush of expectancy fell over the crowd as the leading three moved majestically ahead of their rivals.

With the half-mile time clocked at 1 minute 58.3 seconds, the spectators realised they might soon be part of athletic history. On the third back straight came the critical moment when the 'red comet' Chataway swept ahead. Bannister seemed to falter. Then, above the mounting noise, came the voice of Stampfl: 'Relax.' It brought an immediate response. Bannister obeyed, reaching the three-quarter mark in three minutes. A minute from destiny?

The atmosphere was now electric, the fans ecstatic as Bannister surged into the lead with 250 yards left. His long legs whipping the track from under him, he entered the home straight. His face was strained as he dragged every ounce of energy from his tiring body, but he never lost speed or balance before breaking the tape and collapsing into the arms of Stampfl and an official.

Norris McWhirter added a touch of theatre when he announced: 'Winner of the one mile, R G Bannister, AAA, in a new ground, English native, British native, all-comers, European and world record in a time of 3 minutes …' (McWhirter paused as the crowd screamed in delight) '… 3 minutes 59.4 seconds.'

Bannister was a crumbled heap, held by four strong arms as photographers and spectators clustered around him. 'Did I do it?' he asked. Once recovered, he gave me his own assessment of his triumph: 'I am delighted I achieved this important landmark at the Iffley Road ground, where I ran my first mile seven years ago.' It was a remark typical of Bannister – a man who, despite the Commonwealth and European titles he would go on to win later that year, still wanted to be remembered above all as the part-time athlete and former Oxford student who achieved a landmark mile at home.

The Glorious Twelfth
Duff Hart-Davis

Why should grouse shooting start on August the Twelfth? Strange as it seems when the date is so famous, nobody now seems to know the answer to that. It is true that, even in a year of good weather, the young birds are scarcely mature enough to fly well at the beginning of the month, so that August the First would be too early for kick-off. Equally, September the First would be too late. So maybe the Glorious Twelfth is a compromise.

In any event, the date was laid down by an Act of Parliament in 1773, and although grouse-shooting did not begin on any scale until fifty years later, for the last century and a half the Twelfth has been the most celebrated milestone in the shooting calendar. Even today its approach generates enormous excitement.

The memoirs of the traveller Emily Eden show that by the 1820s English sportsmen were already being attracted to the moors, both in the North of England and in Scotland, which was much harder to reach. Yet it was only with the coming of the railways in the 1840s and 1850s that Scotland became readily accessible and Victorian shooting men began to pour northwards in hordes.

Many a writer extolled the excitement of setting off from London by the evening Limited Mail: the tremendous bustle on the platform at Euston, the crowd of travellers already in their tweeds, the piles of luggage and swarms of dogs, the full-length leather gun-cases, the elaborate picnic hampers thought necessary for survival through the night.

At first grouse were only walked-up – that is, shot by men moving over the moor on foot, either with pointers and setters to detect the birds, or simply advancing in line-abreast. Then came the practice of driving – beaters with flags pushing the coveys forward over the guns ensconced in lines of butts. This, at first, was denounced as grossly unsporting, but soon landowners saw that it was the way to make really worthwhile bags and took it up enthusiastically.

As far as anyone now remembers, no special rituals ever attached to the Twelfth. The exhilaration of the day came from being out on the moors for the first time, full of expectation, with the heather rioting in purple bloom, the weather glorious and cock grouse going off like alarm clocks – *go-back, go-back, go-back* – all round.

Until the Second World War most moors were owned by private individuals, who entertained friends at their own expense. Guests would arrive in total ignorance of prospects for the season: naturally they came hoping for the best, but they had no idea whether the grouse had bred well or not, and to ask their host direct questions was considered scarcely polite. Nowadays things are rather different: with customers flying in from the Continent or America, and paying £100 a brace – £20,000 for a 200-brace day – the owner or manager of the moor must know in advance exactly how he stands, and for this vital information he depends entirely on his gamekeeper.

Here again there has been a profound change. In the old days received wisdom held that any incursion onto the moor in June or July would have a fatally disruptive effect on the coveys of young birds, which would disappear elsewhere if disturbed, and keepers dared not set foot on the hallowed heather before the Twelfth. Now they go out in July and count the birds systematically, working back and forth along each beat with their dogs running free, secure in the knowledge that such manoeuvres cause no disturbance whatever. By this means a good keeper is able to give his boss a precise estimate in advance of the number of grouse his parties will be able to shoot, not merely on the opening day but during the entire season.

One irony of the Twelfth is that the legendary glamour of the occasion is often missing in reality. The weather may be too hot, with the result that the birds do not fly well. The grouse themselves may still be immature. The best shooting almost always comes towards the end of August and in September and October, when the birds are stronger and the weather wilder. It is true that the all-time record bag of 2,929 grouse was made on 12 August 1915, on the Littledale and Abbeystead moors in Lancashire, but most of the great massacres have come later in the season.

Much, of course, depends on the calibre of the people shooting. Driven grouse are notoriously difficult to hit, since they fly extremely fast, hug the contours and make violent changes of direction by merely lifting or dropping one wing. Early in the season they are not so testing; but come late September, when they have grown wily and autumn gales are blowing, they leave inexperienced practitioners groping. Many a keeper, wanting a large bag, has been heard uttering fearful curses at the incompetence of his visitors: records of 500 shots being fired in a drive and fewer than twenty birds killed are all too common.

Every grouse-shooter worth his or her salt has read *The Twelfth*, the farcical novel written by J K Stanford when he was in the army near El Alamein in 1942. The book, which has become a classic, tells how a major moor-bore, George Hysteron-Proteron, 'the stout, baldish little man with the scarlet face', apparently falls asleep and dies in an armchair in his London club, but in fact is transmogrified into a cock grouse. At first he is appalled by his change of identity and by the discomfort of his new environment, with nothing but heather-shoots and grit to eat and only water to drink. But as the shooting season approaches, he realises that he has a chance of settling scores with some of his old human enemies; and on the Twelfth he carefully shepherds the entire stock of grouse from one beat to the next ahead of the shooting party, so that, to their inexpressible chagrin, drive after drive is blank.

The explosive end of the story need not be revealed here: suffice it to say that the novel, though deliberately ridiculous and fantastical, lives and breathes with the author's deep knowledge of the moors and their natural history, and conjures up the spirit and tensions of the great day with a skill no other book can match.

Overleaf: Sitting targets: grouse unaware of the date, 12 August 1935

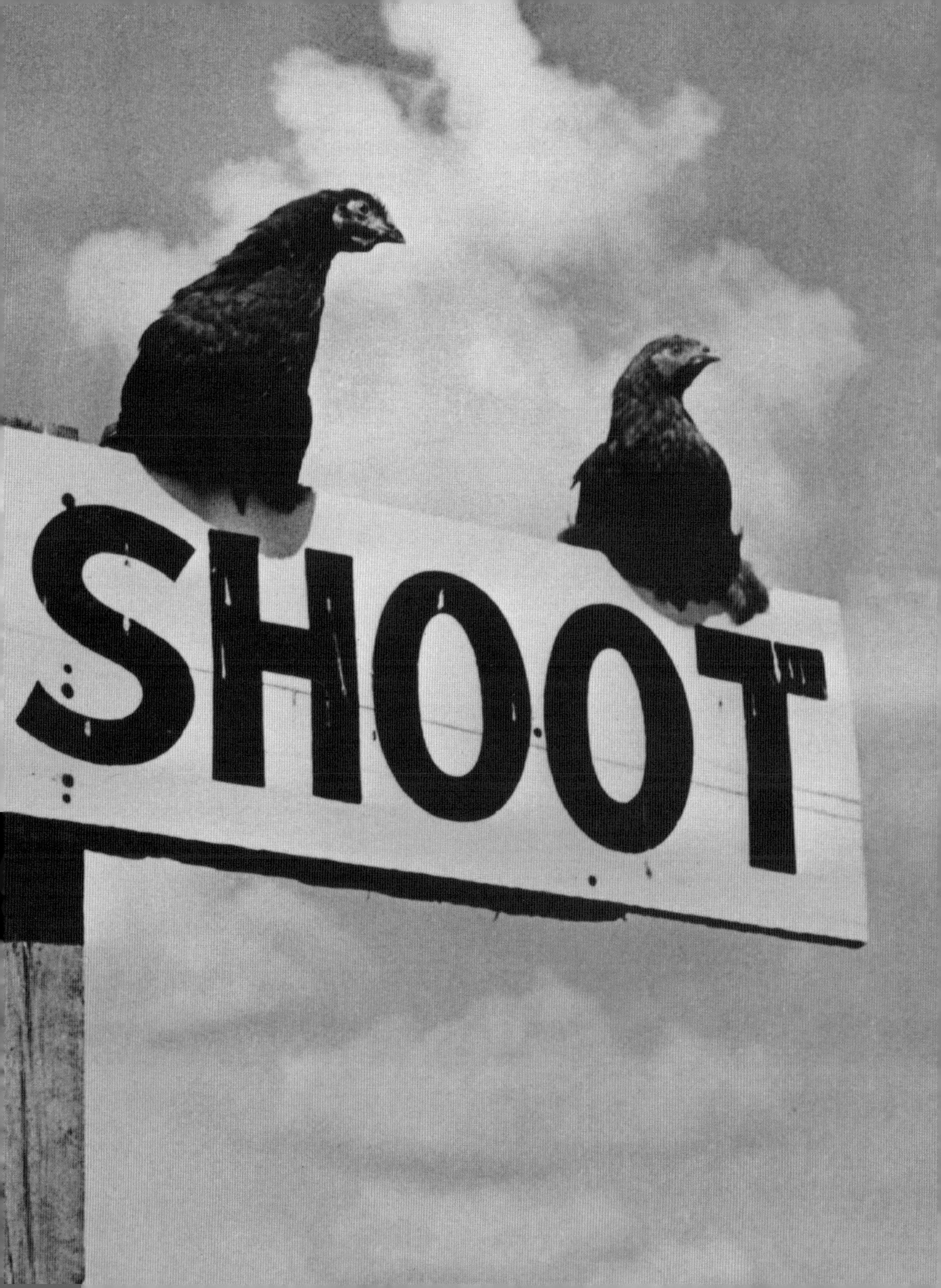
SHOOT

W G Grace: 'The Champion'
Simon Rae

In his Victorian heyday, W G Grace shared a pinnacle of celebrity with royalty, successful generals, explorers and the better known prime ministers. The British Empire spanned the globe; cricket was the Empire's game, and 'WG' was cricket. As the ever-expanding print media spread word of his unprecedented feats around the world, Grace became the first modern sporting superstar. For a comparable figure today we would have to look beyond cricket altogether to a universal icon like Muhammad Ali.

Born in a village backwater on the outskirts of Bristol in 1848, Grace was brought up in a cricket-obsessed family. Two of his four brothers would join him in the England Test team, but WG established his cricketing seniority very early. In 1864 he scored 170 against the Gentlemen of Sussex and followed it with 50 against MCC on his first appearance at Lord's – phenomenal achievements for a teenager. In 1866 he scored his first first-class century – 224 not out – for an England XI v. Surrey at the Oval, and the floodgates opened. He topped the batting averages for seven successive seasons from 1868 to 1874 (in 1871 his average of 78.25 was more than *twice* that of the next batsman) and recorded the highest aggregate for nine successive seasons, from 1869 to 1877. It took him just over ten years to compile his first fifty centuries, which represented a staggering 33 per cent of *all* centuries scored in all first-class cricket in England during the same period. In 1876, he scored cricket's first triple century, closely followed by the second. In one ten-day period he made 344, 177 and 318 not out: 839 runs, average 419.5. Grace was only marginally less successful as a bowler and fielder. He was the first man to do the 'double' of a thousand runs and a hundred wickets, and became, at twenty-eight, the youngest cricketer to reach a thousand first-class wickets. He was equally outstanding as a fielder, taking the most catches every season from 1871 to 1878.

Universally acclaimed as 'The Champion' by his early twenties, Grace dominated the domestic game as no previous cricketer had ever done. The Gentlemen v. Players fixture had long been a one-sided affair, with the Gentlemen winning only seven matches in the thirty-five years before WG made his debut for them. Of the next fifty games they won thirty-one and lost only seven.

Grace also had a huge influence on the politics and structure of the game. In the early 1860s the professionals were in the ascendant. They had formed their own elevens to play lucrative exhibition matches up and down the country, pioneered the even more lucrative overseas tour, and treated the amateur hierarchy at Lord's with a freedom bordering on contempt. Had Grace thrown his lot in with them, the professionals could have declared total independence and gone their own way. However in 1869 MCC

Britain's first sporting superstar: W G Grace at the crease in 1890, by Archibald Wortley

astutely conscripted him and the balance of power shifted. With the greatest crowd-puller of all time among their ranks, Lord's could resume the reins of power. The professionals realised they could not compete and fell into line. The shape of English cricket was determined for the next hundred years and more.

All Grace asked in return was to be allowed to flout the central tenet of the amateur faith: he made more money out of the game than any professional could have dreamed of. His rapacity was most clearly exposed in his negotiations over his two tours to Australia. In 1873–4 he required £1,500 for himself, while paying his professionals £170; in 1891–2 his fee went up to £3,000 plus travel and accommodation for his family. He demanded similar appearance money at home, thinly disguised as 'expenses'. This 'shamateurism' was a running scandal throughout his career, but Grace was untouchable. As the editor of Wisden conceded, quoting *Henry V*: 'nice customs curtsey to great kings'.

Grace was no more compromising on the cricket field and while his ultra-competitive spirit made him a formidable opponent, it led to numberless unsavoury incidents. Perhaps the most significant occurred in the Oval Test of 1882. In attempting to swing this low-scoring, intensely fought cliffhanger by running out one of the Australians who assumed the ball was 'dead', Grace merely managed to provoke the 'Demon' Spofforth into one of the great bowling performances of all time. As a result of Australia's shock victory, the *Sporting Times* published the famous spoof obituary of English cricket with its footnote that 'The body will be cremated and the Ashes taken to Australia'. So the game's greatest trophy came into being largely through the unsporting action of the game's greatest player.

Although Grace was past his first irrepressible flush of youth when Test cricket arrived, he made a spirited 152 on debut and remained England's mainstay for two decades. Overlooked for the captaincy until he was forty, he nevertheless proved a canny and inspirational leader with an almost unbroken run of Ashes victories. He was still opening the batting for England in his fifty-first year.

This longevity is one of the many factors contributing to his greatness. In 1895, at the age of forty-six, he had an Indian summer to compare with any of his earlier triumphs. He became the first man to score a thousand runs before the end of May and also the first batsman to register a hundred first-class centuries. The nation was enthralled and the *Daily Telegraph* set up a national testimonial to which everyone seems to have contributed from the prime minister down to the meanest schoolboy.

When he finally retired in 1908 Grace left the statisticians a mountain of work and to this day there are different versions of his final figures. What are known as the 'traditional' figures are:

Runs: 54,896, average 39.55 with 126 centuries
Wickets: 2,864, average 17.99
Catches: 887

Modern research has uncovered such anomalies as matches in which only WG's figures were given first-class status, and J R Webber in his unparalleled epic *The Chronicle of WG* now offers the following revised figures:

Runs: 54,211, average 39.45 with 124 centuries
Wickets: 2,808, average 18.15
Catches: 876

Grace's Test record was: matches 22, innings 36, not out 2, highest score 170, runs 1,098, average 32.29. He took nine wickets at 26.22 and thirty-nine catches. He captained England on thirteen occasions, winning eight, losing two and drawing three.

Though never knighted or accorded any other public recognition, apart from the Grace Gates at Lord's, WG was firmly ensconced in the national consciousness. When in 1915 he died as a result of a heart attack brought on by Zeppelin raids over his South London home, the news briefly pushed the carnage of the trenches off the front pages. For his contemporaries, as for subsequent generations, the huge bearded face surmounted by the seemingly too-small cap proved the strongest and most enduring symbol of the national game.

Henley Regatta
Daniel Topolski

Henley Royal Regatta is Mecca for rowers worldwide: an eccentric, quintessentially English sporting event that combines a high-level international competition with the atmosphere of an Edwardian garden party. It is the sort of occasion that the British feel they can organise better than anyone else; and that success is demonstrated by the fact that it attracts bigger crowds than any other rowing event.

Henley used to be a crucial date in the frenetic diary of the debutante's 'London season' and while it still takes its place, as June gives way to July, in the midsummer social calendar after Ascot and before Wimbledon Finals day, Cowes and Glyndebourne, its organisers have, since the mid-1980s, ensured the participation of the world's best rowers by judiciously offering financial assistance for travel and accommodation.

At first glance, you could be forgiven for thinking that the frolicking champagne- and Pimms-swilling revellers inside the exclusive Steward's Enclosure, or along the towpath of the one-mile-and-550-yard course, were the only focus of Henley. But you would be mistaken, even though the first day or two of racing, while providing some bravely fought head-to-head battles, suggests a low level of competition, with unfancied schools, colleges and club crews fighting for the chance to meet their seeded (selected) rivals in one of the nineteen designated events. These favourites only really begin to break sweat in the quarter-finals.

But on the Friday, the third day of racing, the big international players take centre stage and the real class of this five-day Thames-side festival becomes apparent. Olympic and World champions demonstrate what high-level rowing is really about, as Britain's national team attempts to defend the top Open titles against the best of their overseas rivals – the crews they will meet a few weeks later at the World Rowing Championships or the Olympics.

Why do the top stars want to come? Because to take part at Henley is special. It is as different from the usual international circuit as it could possibly be. It is one thing to race six abreast on a custom-built, buoyed 2,000-metre course, with the spectators sitting in grandstands set way back from the water's edge. But nothing in rowing, except perhaps the Olympic Games, comes close to Henley on Finals day: the claustrophobic, head-to-head, knockout competition within its electric arena-like atmosphere, racing between the two sets of solid, unforgiving wooden booms which demarcate the course – and which have proved the undoing of even experienced steersmen – all in front of a Steward's Enclosure crowd cheering you on just a few feet away during the last 200 yards to the finish. From the high-tension moments of quiet calm at the start, alongside Temple Island,

A Steward's Enclosure badge at Henley, a Mecca for rowers worldwide

to the explosive roar at the finish, it is an unforgettable experience and one that I have thrilled to repeat seventy-six times during a thirty-year career.

Then there is the elaborate silverware to be won, the verdicts given traditionally in feet, lengths, canvases and 'Easily's instead of fractions of seconds. And the rules: men in ties and jackets no matter how hot it is and women refused entry if they dare to wear slacks or a hemline above the knee. But what a treat for visiting Russian and Egyptian Olympians to see the profusion of boaters, summer frocks and college blazers punting by.

Sir Steve Redgrave, the dyslexic builder's son from nearby Marlow and one of the world's greatest athletes, has made Henley his spiritual home, winning twenty titles since he first competed there in 1980 – the last a year after his official retirement from the sport following his astonishing fifth successive Olympic Gold Medal in Sydney.

Yet despite Redgrave's exceptional record, he is not the most successful Henley competitor. That honour goes to Guy Nichalls, who between 1885 and 1907 notched up twenty-two titles, and F S Gulston, with twenty-one between 1868 and 1880; but Redgrave lost only three of his sixty-nine races to Nichalls' ten from seventy appearances.

The inaugural regatta was in 1839, when the local mayor and townsfolk decided to capitalise on the huge success of the first Oxford and Cambridge Boat Race, which was held at Henley ten years earlier. There were just three events – the Grand Challenge Cup for eights, the Town Cup for fours and a sculling race for watermen – contested on one afternoon by, for the most part, colleges from Oxford and Cambridge.

Within eight years it was an annual two-day festival with eleven events. In 1886 it was extended to three days and by 1906 it was a four-day extravaganza; in 1986, with ever-increasing events and entrants, it grew to five. But not until 1993 were women allowed to compete, with a women's sculling race added to the programme; an event for 'eights' and one for quadruple sculls were added in 1999 and 2001. The overall number of entries has doubled since the 1970s to well over 500, a fifth of whom come from abroad.

Ed Smith from New York was the first overseas athlete to compete – in the Diamond Sculls – in 1872; but the first winners were Colombia University, who carried the Visitors' Fours trophy back to America in 1878. And it was an American too who was at the heart of one of the most controversial episodes in the regatta's history. Grace Kelly's father John fell foul of the notorious and élitist 'manual labourer' rule and was barred from competing in the Diamond Sculls because he was alleged to have been an apprentice bricklayer in his youth. Rowing was for 'gentlemen' only.

The offending regulation was eventually dropped in 1938 and Kelly returned in 1947 with his son Jack, who avenged his father's humiliation by winning the coveted title. Thirty-four years later, Princess Grace demonstrated that the Kellys no longer bore any grudge when she presented the prizes. But first she was able to watch, in the pouring rain, one of the most spectacular races ever seen at Henley as my Oxford University/Thames Tradesmen crew came from a length behind to defeat the British National eight in the Grand Challenge Cup – the first Oxford victory in the regatta's premier event for 128 years.

Little has changed since those early Edwardian days. The main differences now are that the operation is slicker and the budget much bigger, while the best of the competing athletes are amongst the best trained in the world in any sport. But as always, mixing in amongst those frolicking 'social circuit' funsters are rowing's old-timers, reliving the adrenalin rush of their glory days – their equivalent of Wimbledon's Centre Court or Wembley on Cup Final day. Another chance to get a taste of that exhilarating high and to soak up again the smell and the feel that once gave them such intense pleasure, such dignity and at times such heartache.

The Highland Games
Geoff Capes

There is a film called *Wee Geordie*, starring Bill Travers as a Scottish gamekeeper's son who, by dint of a bodybuilding course and much training, becomes a world-class hammer-thrower. One scene has always had a particular resonance for me. It takes place at the Olympics. Travers is about to make his last throw of the hammer, on which his winning – and a world record – depends. As he stands there, on the brink of success or failure, he drifts into a dream, thinking back to the Highlands and the Highland Games and longing to return to them. Whenever I see it, I feel I was that man.

I dabbled in the Games as a youngster, but it was only after many years of competing in track and field events, and being reasonably successful in winning British, Commonwealth and European championships, that I discovered them in earnest. I was looking around for a new challenge in life, another sport to follow in order to lengthen my sporting career. And it was then that the world of the Highland Games really opened up to me.

There is no other event in the sporting calendar quite like the Highland Games. Older in origin than the modern Olympics, the Games began as a meeting place for the clans to show off their fighting skills. They owe their enduring popularity, though, to the revival of interest in Highland culture fostered by Sir Walter Scott and his like in the early nineteenth century. Held annually at a number of locations through the Highlands, the Games consist of five disciplines: the stone; the twenty-eight pound for distance; the hammer; the fifty-six pound for height; and the caber (from the Gaelic *cabar*, meaning pole). These are all supreme trials of throwing strength, no doubt based on the tests of physical prowess working men used to set one another in times gone by. The hammer, for example, probably derives from competitions among blacksmiths, quarrymen or farmhands to see who could throw the tools of their trade the furthest. More obscure are the origins of the caber – a wooden pole anything up to 70kgs (150lbs) in weight and 5.3m (19ft 9ins) in length (though the longest ever recorded was apparently a staggering 127kg (280lbs) and 7.62m (25ft)) – but it may be a sport invented by foresters. However it began, 'tossing the caber' is probably the first image that comes into people's minds when they think of the Highland Games today.

To begin with, even for me as an experienced Olympian, these disciplines were hard to learn, but I was determined to succeed. Before anything else, though, my first job was to get myself a kilt. Being an Englishman, I felt that the only tartan I could wear so as not to claim descent in any way was the Royal Stewart. (Only later did my researches show that I actually had Scottish blood all along – going back to 1190, in fact – so I could have worn my own tartan after all.)

Once I set my mind to acquiring the new skills required by the Games I learnt very fast, and before long I was challenging the best in the field: the great Bill Anderson, Grant

Anderson and of course Hamish Davidson, to name but a few. But wherever I went the real competition became England versus Scotland.

At first the change from the world of putting the shot came as a bit of a shock. The new regime could hardly have been more different. I had been used to travelling the world, staying in nice comfy hotels wherever I went. Now I drove up from my home in Lincolnshire to my base in Blackford in Perthshire every Friday evening, competed on Saturday and Sunday, and then headed back south again on the Sunday evening. This made for a journey of approximately 900 miles each weekend for about sixteen weeks at a stretch. But I loved the additional challenge.

Of the numerous events which go to make up the Highland Games, the one most people talked about, then as now, was the Braemar Games. These are the ones attended by the Royal Family – Queen Victoria was the first to put in an appearance at them, in 1848 – and it is the Braemar Games I still remember most fondly. Nor is it only the sporting side of things that stays in my mind. I vividly recall one occasion when I was presented with the Braemar Trophy by the Queen. I had not had time to wash the 'sticky' off my hands after the event – 'sticky' is the resin used by competitors to prevent the wooden shafts of the hammer and the caber slipping when you throw them – and after receiving the Trophy I found myself stuck to Her Majesty's hand. Fortunately, everyone saw the funny side, including the Royal Family themselves – and I still have the photo to prove it!

There will always be a special place in my heart for the Highland Games – for their inimitable combination of fun and laughter, friends, foes, beautiful scenery, and all the colour of an event steeped in history and tradition. There is nothing to match that atmosphere: the Highland dancers of all ages, the pipe bands, the cycling, the fell-running, the Cumberland wrestling, the tug o' war. Above all, though, it is the sheer honesty of the Games that I remember most fondly.

Yes, I can understand Wee Geordie's longing only too well.

Oh and by the way, he won with that last throw.

A contestant prepares to throw at the Aboyne Highland Games, 1933

The partnership of Hobbs and Sutcliffe
Mihir Bose

Cricket is a team game built round a myriad of individual contests between bat and ball, what Sir Neville Cardus called the play within a play. This is most riveting when great pairs are at work: great pairs of fast bowlers, spinners or batsmen.

Such partnerships resonate beyond the game, but there is nothing quite as fascinating as watching a great opening pair in action. The fact that eleven men can toil on the field and not even take an opposition wicket has an irresistible attraction, while being utterly soul-destroying for the fielding side.

John Berry (Jack, later Sir Jack) Hobbs and Herbert Sutcliffe's opening partnerships for England between the two world wars left such an indelible memory that they are almost universally seen as the finest opening partnership in all of cricket history. Their record has been statistically challenged since then, but they remain the template of opening pairs.

The truly astonishing thing about their achievements is that they batted together for England in a mere twenty-six Tests, spread over six years. Yet in fifteen of these Tests the pair put on stands of over a hundred runs. But more than the runs they scored, it was the manner in which they made them, and the fact that their batting almost single-handedly revived English cricket after the First World War, that gives them such a unique status.

Consider the context. It is almost six years since the end of the most devastating war the world has ever seen. English life is recovering, but it seems England will never again be able to master Australia in cricket. Australia, less affected by the war, has produced such an awesome team that between December 1920 and January 1925 they win eleven of their thirteen Tests against England, at one stage winning eight Tests in succession.

It is against this dismal background that in December 1924 Hobbs and Sutcliffe started opening the innings against Australia. In their very first Test at Sydney they put on 157 in the first and 110 in the second innings. It could not stop Australia winning. Australia also won the second Test, but Hobbs and Sutcliffe put on 283 and the pair batted throughout the third day, the first such instance in Test history. Their batting was the foundation for the long hoped-for England fight-back, which came on 18 February 1925 when, for the first time since 1912, England beat Australia in a Test. Hobbs and Sutcliffe put on 126 for the first wicket and, after Hobbs was out for 66, Sutcliffe went on to make 143 in a match-winning England score of 548. The Ashes were already lost, but the tide was beginning to turn.

It finally turned in August 1926 when, in a memorable match at the Oval, England regained the Ashes, after fourteen years, defeating Australia by 289 runs. The previous

The finest opening partnership in cricket history: Jack Hobbs and Herbert Sutcliffe

four Tests had been drawn. The first innings of this Test, which was made timeless to get a result, had seen the two sides virtually level-pegging. England had made 280, Hobbs and Sutcliffe putting on 53, Australia 302. On the Monday evening the pair put on 49, then overnight there was a violent thunderstorm over the Oval and the wicket the next day was spiteful. But Hobbs and Sutcliffe batted as if they had rolled out their own special wicket. They put on 172, Hobbs making 100, his first against Australia at his home ground, and Sutcliffe 161, and the England score of 436 was the launch pad for Wilfred Rhodes and

Harold Larwood to bowl England to one of their finest victories over the old enemy.

It was this match-winning partnership in the most daunting of circumstances that created the enduring legend. In that series Hobbs and Sutcliffe put on 32 (unfinished), 182, 59, 156, 58 and finally 172. Cardus, who had been critical of the pair during the series, often castigating them for slow cricket, was now in raptures and wrote the next day in the *Guardian*: 'These performances, coming after the men's greatness in Australia, must leave us silent with admiration and gratitude. Shall we ever look upon the like of Hobbs and Sutcliffe again?'

As a partnership, they would have two more series against Australia. The 1928–9 series in Australia was crucial. This saw the emergence of a certain Donald Bradman. England easily won the first two Tests and Hobbs and Sutcliffe as a pair did nothing much. But when England looked in trouble in the third at Melbourne they came into their own. Bradman made 100, England on a rain-affected wicket were set 332 to win. Once again Hobbs and Sutcliffe showed that the greater the challenge, the better they responded. The pair were out on 105, Sutcliffe going on to make 135 to ensure a three-wicket victory, which meant the Ashes were retained. There would be one more century stand in Australia and two more in England in 1930, but by then Hobbs, now forty-eight, was ready to bow out of Test cricket and leave the stage to Bradman.

Cricketing partnerships of this kind are nearly always between men of similar ages. But Hobbs was already forty-two when he opened with Sutcliffe, who was thirty, for the first time – on 14 June 1924 at Edgbaston against South Africa, starting with a century stand. For Hobbs the partnership came during his second cricketing period, the one after the First World War, and he always wanted to be remembered for his batting before the war, when he felt he was more adventurous. The war also delayed Sutcliffe's entry into cricket. He was twenty-four when he first played for Yorkshire in 1919. At county level both men had partners who in another age might have played more often for England: Andy Sandham with Hobbs at Surrey and Percy Holmes with Sutcliffe at Yorkshire.

Of Hobbs' genius as a cricketer there can be no doubt. G H Hardy, the Cambridge mathematician, used to rank the most difficult mathematical problems as 'in the Hobbs class'. Sutcliffe as a batsman was perhaps not in the Hobbs class, but he was always the man for the big occasion. His Test average is higher than his county one, and he knew that rare secret, that mastery comes to the man who knows his technical limitations.

The moment he batted with Sutcliffe, Hobbs had no doubt he had found his ideal partner. It came against Australia. Kellaway, who swung the ball late, bowled the opening over. Hobbs withdrew his bat at the last minute, but he knew what he was doing looked risky. At the end of the over Sutcliffe walked down the wicket and said 'I think I'd leave them alone, Jack, if I were you'. Hobbs would later tell Cardus: 'Then I knew we'd found the right opener for England.'

James Hunt
Stephen Bayley

People say they remember Kennedy and Lennon, but for me it is James Hunt. I was driving home along the King's Road on a summer evening in 1993 when I heard the six o'clock news on the car radio. The curiously youthful Hunt had died of a sudden heart attack. It was 15 June and he was forty-five. I scarcely knew him, but felt I had lost a real friend, a great collaborator in the war against pomposity. 'It's called a *memento mori*, Murray,' I could almost hear him scornfully say in his relaxed and mischievous Home Counties drawl.

It being the early Nineties, I was working in Chelsea and driving an Audi 80 Quattro, which I felt was all frightfully smart. The ex-Formula One World Champion, on the other hand, was living somewhat reclusively in suburban Wimbledon and driving (apparently still with brio) an Austin A35 van not yet rescued from automobile obscurity by acceptance as an ironic classic. In contrast, the rather grand S-Class Mercedes he had bought with his race winnings was sitting supported by bricks, wheel-less and spattered with bird shit, on the SW19 shingle. This self-conscious symbol of insouciance and neglect was typical of the man. I also gather they found the house was full of budgies. While the tabloids had Hunt filed under playboy, he was always more of an English eccentric with, I suspect, a darker side to his matey bonhomie.

He was also the very last racing driver of his type. There are two images of James Hunt I specially enjoy. The first I saw on television. It was one of his Formula Three races, probably at Brands Hatch at some time in the early 1970s. Hunt had acquired a not wholly unjustified reputation as inclined to crash his cars while travelling very quickly indeed. This he had done, collecting another car and driver in his dramatic on-camera excursus. There, in front of an audience of millions, Hunt got out of the car and elegantly thumped his astonished competitor, decking him.

The next image is a photograph I keep in one of my commonplace books. In an age when racing drivers have personal dieticians, eat wholemeal pasta and salad, have resident personal trainers and think a whiff of ozone is a Baudelairean debauch, it is wonderfully refreshing – inspiring even – to look at Hunt, handsome and wholly dishevelled with his long blond hair, wearing the victor's laurels in a Grand Prix, signing autographs while pulling hard on a Marlboro King Size. Some of the wilder rumours about his sybaritic lifestyle may be a vicious calumny, but it is certainly true that James Hunt had an attitude to his chosen sport that was, to put it no higher, relaxed by contemporary standards.

The Wellington-educated Hunt was one of those apparently easygoing Englishmen who found sport easy. But this was a gentlemanly deception: he played squash to county standard and was, at his best, much more competent and very much more competitive than he ever let on. No one gets to finish a single lap in a Formula One car without being extremely brave, prodigiously talented and amazingly fit. Here Hunt's record speaks for itself: 179 points from ninety-three starts, fourteen pole positions and ten wins. Curmudgeons will say that Hunt never would have become World Champion in 1976 had it not been for Niki Lauda's apocalyptic sidelining crash, but that is in what-if territory. The fact is that on the road that year Hunt beat Lauda. And besides, while no one ever accused the Austrian of being cowardly, he surrendered to the weather in the deciding Japanese Grand Prix while Hunt drove on with manic style and fearlessness.

But there was something romantically fragile about Hunt's achievement. 1976 was a bright, transient peak. For all his speed and courage, his well-spoken recklessness and his sublimely professional amateurism, the fiend that drove him retired as soon as the Championship was won. The James Hunt of the 1977, 1978 and 1979 seasons was demotivated and successively disillusioned. He finished fifth for McLaren in '77, a lamentable thirteenth for the same team the following year. He then joined Walter Wolf's new team and failed even to finish the season. Sex and drugs may, as some said, have played their part in this sad decline, but Hunt stopped being a racing driver because, the Championship won, he realised he was becoming a charming anachronism. He became World Champion at the very last moment the title was available to someone of his inclinations and breeding.

And then, following an ill-advised experiment with farming, he reinvented himself as a commentator for the BBC. Against the demented blather of Murray Walker, Hunt presented a magnificent and utterly English foil. He was witty, laid-back, sadistic, ironic and knowledgeable. Hunt made race commentary into a minor and beguiling art form: his merciless humour animated even the dullest event and turned the noisy glory of racing into a sophisticated *conversazione*. He was reaching an idiosyncratic peak of refinement when his heart stopped.

Perhaps James Hunt had lived more than one life in his forty-five years, but it is pleasant to think that, so far as our imaginations are concerned, he will never grow old. Indeed, the prim always thought him puerile and immature, and to confirm their prejudices Hunt drank and smoked and got the women with regularity and abandon. When he raced for his friend (Lord) Alexander Hesketh, later Government Chief Whip in the Lords, champagne was their primary fuel. Hunt gave Hesketh his first and only win, and in the definitively butch world of motor sport the pair of them used a teddy bear as their irreverent mascot.

When I first met James Hunt it was on a plane from Malaga. He was wearing shorts and a torn T-shirt and dirty loafers. That was in 1979, his retirement year. When I last met him, just before he died, he was wearing shorts, a frugally faded denim shirt and (I am certain they were) the very same dirty loafers. On each occasion he was detached but engaging; humorous, certainly, but with a hint of steel beneath a floppy and foppy surface. Some of this was affectation; most of it was pure style. James Hunt ran his extraordinary life at relaxed speed. He was the last of his sort, a genuine sporting great.

A playboy with a hint of steel: James Hunt preparing to race, 1975

The hunt
Rupert Isaacson

The Victorian novelist and social commentator Anthony Trollope, writing before the advent of mass spectator sports such as football, called fox-hunting the English sport. Since its invention in the 1750s by the Leicestershire squire Hugo Meynell (who founded the Quorn, the first proper fox-hunt as we know it), the hunt field had become firmly established as the place where a young blood won his spurs. Fast, dangerous, and demanding an almost mystical union between man, horse and hound, fox-hunting was new, fashionable and utterly English.

Until Meynell's day mounted hunting had been a very different affair, and one of Norman origin. It mostly involved the pursuit of big game (red deer or wild boar) in big forests, a slow, laborious process called hunting *par force*. Different types of hound (lymiers and talbots for scent, alaunts for aggression and drive) were set on in relays from soon after dawn until the beast was either caught or got away clean. This medieval type of hunting, whose rules and etiquette were codified as early as the tenth century AD, is still practised in modern-day France.

But by the early eighteenth century in Britain most of the big medieval forests had been felled, as England emerged as a maritime power and began turning its timber into ships. Moreover, the old feudal lordship system had in most areas given way to yeoman, or middle-class, farmers. These two factors combined to produce a changed landscape of small woods and private farms whose fields were fenced with hedges or timber or dry-stone walls. Big game was no more. Instead the eighteenth-century squires and yeoman farmers began to hunt hare and, increasingly, fox, across the open fields.

At first they stuck to the old ways, using the same melodious but slow hounds that their forefathers had hunted with in the forests; going out at dawn, keeping the jumping to a minimum and emphasising the kill. But Hugo Meynell and his landed contemporaries, such as Peter Beckford of Dorset and the Pelhams of Lincolnshire, changed all that. They realised that foxes, if hunted at mid-morning, have digested their night's meal and are then willing to run far and fast to elude hounds. This inevitably involved jumping and other derring-do in the saddle. Almost overnight the primary objective of hunting changed from the kill to the chase.

Faster quarry required faster hounds. Meynell and co. began to experiment with crossing the leaner types of old hound with greyhound blood, eventually coming up with a prototype of the modern foxhound – an athletic, aggressive creature with good scenting ability. And to keep up with these hounds the mid-eighteenth-century hunt masters began using the (also newly created) English thoroughbred horses, which could not only run all day but fly whatever obstacles they encountered, thus allowing the huntsman to stay in close contact with his hounds.

The dangerous, adrenalin-fuelled nature of this kind of hunt quickly caught on. By the Regency period anyone who didn't ride hard to hounds, risking life and limb in the process, was considered 'slow'. Mounted fields of fashionable young 'swells' and 'thrusters' vied to out-ride each other, often to the chagrin of the huntsman, who feared his hounds might be trampled upon. This was the golden age of the 'Shires' – as the packs of modern Leicestershire and Northamptonshire (the Quorn, Belvoir, Cottesmore, Fernie, Pytchley and Grafton hunts) are still referred to. Beau Brummel hunted with them. So did the Prince Regent until he got too fat, establishing a tradition of royal fox-hunting that still continues. Cavalry officers were expected to hunt as part of their training. By the early 1900s the sport had become ubiquitous in England, Scotland, Wales and Ireland. Today very few areas of rural Great Britain are without their local hunt.

Perhaps paradoxically, given its feudal roots, the hunt field became one of the few areas of British life where class barriers actually broke down (albeit temporarily), and people from all backgrounds united in a common passion. Though often run by aristocrats (notably the Dukes of Beaufort and Rutland and the Earls of Yarborough, Fitzwilliam and Berkeley), hunts allowed anyone to join as long as they could pay a season's subscription or daily 'cap'. Moreover, for every pack run by blue-bloods there was a local farmers' or town pack run by committee or a set of joint-masters – a system that has become the norm today. Prince or tradesman, you rode as well as your skill allowed. On the hunt field, if not elsewhere in Victorian society, a democratic spirit was actively encouraged.

As with all the great British sports, fox-hunting was also soon exported. Today, there are as many hunts in the USA and Canada as in the UK, and Australia and New Zealand both have thriving hunt scenes. Hunting also gave rise to the modern sports of point-to-point racing and steeplechasing, which began with men, while riding home from hunting, challenging each other to ride straight at a steeple on the horizon, jumping whatever they found in their way.

Today, hunting has never been more popular, with 185 registered foxhound packs in Britain alone. At the same time it has never been more abhorred. One of the great British political dramas of the last hundred years has been the campaign to abolish hunting. The sight of hunt saboteurs racing across country in balaclavas, pursuing a hunt that is in turn pursuing a fox has become as quintessentially British a scene as the hunt itself.

'So hault! Il est hault!' – the stag is up – cried our Norman ancestors as they pursued the beast through the forests outside London (today's Soho). 'Tally Ho!' cry the huntsmen of today when they see a fox break covert. 'Bastards!' cry the hunt sabs, before setting off in hot pursuit. Clearly, the urge to hunt is so deeply embedded in our national psyche that now, in the twenty-first century, tens of thousands of people still turn out several days a week from September to March to hurl themselves across country in excited pursuit of an elusive, fast-running quarry. Whether hunting the fox or hunting the hunt, it is the same spirit which guides them.

Overleaf: *In pursuit of the uneatable:* Through the Gate *by John Frederick Herring (1815–1907)*

Voices of cricket: John Arlott and Brian Johnston
Christopher Martin-Jenkins

For a dozen years – it seemed much, much longer – radio listeners in Britain and the Commonwealth with even the slightest interest in cricket had the opportunity to enjoy a partnership as engaging in its field as Flanagan and Allen, Morecambe and Wise or the Two Ronnies. In the case of one of the pair the analogy is not inapt, because Brian Johnston would have liked nothing better than to have been a stand-up comic. He was a born entertainer, whether there was a microphone in front of him or not. Whether you were listening to him on the air or enjoying his company in person, his gift was to make people smile.

'Johnners', as all his many friends knew him, had followed Eton with a brief period in the City, far too small a square mile for his personality. After winning an MC at Arnhem, he started after the war as a radio broadcaster of events and topical programmes, but he made his reputation in cricket on television.

John Arlott, who commentated on cricket from 1946 after years in local government and as a copper on the beat in his native Hampshire, was an altogether more serious man, a poet and philosopher. His imagination ran deeper, so he sometimes foresaw and tended to linger on life's sorrows. He wore a black tie for the last thirty years of his life in memory of the son to whom he had given as a twenty-first birthday present the sports car in which he later killed himself. He enjoyed a hearty laugh as much as the next man, but in the wee small hours, if the previous evening's generous intake of food and wine had not had its calming effect, his mind no doubt turned to questions of eternity. Brian's would have dwelt instead on the story of the vicar and the parrot, or the man at the bus-stop with a banana in his ear.

To a large extent their broadcasting styles reflected their characters: Brian's as light and pleasing as a cheese soufflé; John's as deep and many-faceted as the clarets he adored. There was, however, a paradox in their styles when it came to describing the events of a cricket match, ball by ball, day after day. It was Arlott who to some extent gave the oratorical performance; Johnners who just projected himself, one of the most natural communicators in broadcasting history.

Arlott, mind you, made no effort to disguise his relatively humble origins. Perhaps the war, and the success of the likes of J B Priestley and Wilfred and Mabel Pickles, had paved the way for regional accents. He spoke in a Hampshire burr that gained immediate acceptance at a time when BBC voices were still almost exclusively confined to the type of Oxford English personified by John Snagge. Arlott's drawl grew deeper and slower with age, but the style never altered: with an easy command of words and brilliant timing (the secret of success in most walks of life) he set out to paint a complete and vivid picture of all that happened on the field, always with an eye on the weather and a fine appreciation

of the nuances of the cricket and the character and appearance of the players. He had a
wonderful sense of the human drama of the game, and no one knew better how to use
the dramatic pause:

> Lindwall's shirt fills with wind as he runs in, arms pumping, and bowls to
> Hutton … [pause] … It's an out-swinger … [slightly longer pause –
> applause from crowd] … and Hutton strokes him through the covers for
> four quite gloriously … [lingering emphasis on the last word; longer pause
> still] … 38 for no wicket, Hutton 21. Lindwall turns at the Vauxhall End,
> medium height, muscular of build, runs smoothly in again, bowls to
> Hutton … [pause] … an in-swinger … [longest pause yet] … and Hutton
> is bowled … Hutton bowled Lindwall … 21.

Johnston, by contrast, was bubbly and convivial. His listener truly felt like the chap in
the seat next to him. He simply described all he saw in an easily accessible, conversational
style, with a quick eye for anything unusual happening in amongst the crowd or outside
the ground, especially if he could get a laugh out of it.

He changed with social convention, becoming, like the BBC itself, increasingly
informal: what would have been 'a lady in a blue frock eating an ice cream' in his
television commentaries of the 1950s had become simply 'a woman munching rather a
tasty-looking choc-ice' by the time he had inherited from Arlott the title of the 'Voice of
Cricket' in the 1980s. Although he kept strictly to the essential rules of commentary, laid
down in writing for all exponents of the craft by the head of outside broadcasts, Seymour
de Lotbiniere – basic information such as who was bowling to whom from what end of
the ground and where that was in relation to the commentary position – he always felt
free to range far and wide, working in stories of what had happened to him on his way to
the ground that morning, or the fact that his little Yorkshire terrier, Minnie, had 'been
having a little trouble with the waterworks' and was on the way to the vet. Thus were
listeners drawn into his personal life. They knew where he lived, what his wife Pauline had
been doing to brighten up the garden and what the umpires had said to him when he
popped into their dressing-room before the start of play.

He became, more than anyone else, a friendly voice in the room for the woman
working in the kitchen or the lorry driver on his way up the motorway. One by one his
colleagues in the commentary box became familiar too. Scorers had once been
disembodied voices occasionally chipping in with a bowler's analysis or the details of a
record fourth-wicket partnership; but now Bill Frindall was christened 'the bearded
wonder' and encouraged to join in or react to Brian's puns, while the 'expert summarisers'
like Freddie Brown, Trevor Bailey and Fred Trueman gradually started to comment
during an over rather than at the end of it.

If Arlott satisfied the cricketing connoisseurs, Johnston was mainly responsible for
popularising *Test Match Special* and building up the programme's cult status during the
years on Radio Three when the wavelength's controller, the Austrian-born Stephen

Hearst, described cricket commentary as 'an art form'.

   Having both mixed television and radio commentaries for some years, Johnston and Arlott finally came together as part of the ball-by-ball radio commentary team in 1969, and from the following season, although they usually dined in separate company when stumps were drawn, they were inseparable during what may be remembered as the golden years of the 1970s.

   Arlott retired at the end of the 1980 season, escaping his public life by moving to Alderney in the Channel Islands. He had virtually worn himself out with a heavy writing load on top of his broadcasting, and one day in that final summer, after mixing pills

'Johnners': Brian Johnston in 1962

prescribed by his doctor with his usual almost pint-sized glass of claret before lunch, he fell asleep in front of the microphone immediately after giving his usual immaculate description of play in the last twenty minutes of the morning and handing over to Fred Trueman for his comments. A few weeks later he eschewed any dramatic farewell and left his listeners with the words: 'And after a word from Trevor Bailey, it'll be Christopher Martin-Jenkins.'

Brian never retired. He was still the life and soul of *Test Match Special*, and still travelling the country delighting theatre audiences with a one-man show about his life to raise money for his grandchildren's education, when in 1994 he had the heart attack from which he never recovered.

A poet of the airwaves: John Arlott in 1955

Jousting
Rupert Isaacson

Ever since the mythical King Arthur pulled the sword from the stone, jousts, tournaments, battles and quests have been fundamental to our idea of merrie Englande, the British past. And although jousting pundits and medievalists have long disputed whether it was the Norman Brits or the Norman French who actually invented the joust, certainly the ferocious match between two armoured men, mounted and armed with heavy lances, is part of our national myth.

The word 'joust' derives from the Latin *juxtae*, which means 'coming together' (think 'junction' or 'juncture') and jousting may be a descendant of the Roman 'Game of Troy', a series of mounted contests between young aristocratic citizens – which the Romans had in their turn taken from the Greeks. It is also known that the Germanic tribes who overran the Roman Empire (and eventually settled England) played rough mounted games with lances. To do so they used a piece of clever technology that had originated in Central Asia – the stirrup – which enabled a mounted man to absorb the shock of a lance connecting with another man, instead of being sent in a somersault over his horse's rear.

By the early medieval period – the eighth to tenth centuries – tournaments involving mounted knights using lances, swords and just about anything else that came to hand had become ubiquitous in Europe. Local barons settled disputes this way, and they also offered young knights a chance to win money and favour. However, they were chaotic affairs – mini-wars that sprawled across whole districts and went on for days – which tended to be hard on the local inhabitants, as well as wasteful of noble life. Because of this, several popes passed bulls excommunicating those who took part in mass-tournaments. Some bishops refused Christian burial to those killed in them. And some kings – including England's Henry II and Edward III – uneasy at the political implications of large numbers of armoured men fighting willy-nilly over the countryside, tried unsuccessfully to ban them.

As time went on, however, the emphasis became more and more on single combat. The first known set of rules governing such a joust (or tilt – from the old English word *tealte* – to fall) were codified in Normandy in 1066 by one Godfroi de Preuilly. Ironically, this unlucky Norman was killed during the very tournament he had organised, but the Normans quickly made jousting their own. On the British side of the Channel, further rules and refinements were developed during the reign of King Stephen, in the early 1100s, and these continued throughout the Middle Ages. The 1292 Statute of Arms dictated that lances must be tipped with a 'coronal' (little crown) instead of a point, so as not to penetrate armour. Special jousting helms – with long slits for a wider view – came

A tournament of knights before Richard II: an illustration from the 15th-century St Albans Chronicle

into vogue, and later, with the development of plate armour, came breastplates designed to burst apart spectacularly upon being struck. Professional jousters, who went from tournament to tournament all over Europe, became a feature of medieval society (as in Chaucer's 'Knight's Tale' and the recent film of the same name). Every city had jousting clubs, or orders, for aristocrats and the richer merchants, which sponsored the tournaments and laid on the pageantry.

In the early fourteenth century the Duke of Gloucester, a kind of medieval Queensberry, codified the rules still further. Tilting grounds were to be sixty paces by forty, fenced all round, with exits at the east and west sides. Lances were weakened so that they would shatter on heavy impact. A barrier was set up between the two riders so that they had to hit each other at an angle (safer than a head-on collision). Jousters had to aim for the boss, or the four nails, on their opponent's shield. Sometimes the helm or gorget (throat armour) was also a permissible target. Appointed marshals decided all results, and their decision was final. To make the process more romantic, ladies' favours could also be worn. Of course, this was assuming that one was jousting *à plaisance* (for sport). Until the mid-sixteenth century jousting *à l'outrance* (to the death, with non-modified weapons) remained a way for nobles to settle disputes, usually with paid champions doing the dirty work. Most jousts were purely sporting, however.

But even with the new, safer methods, death and serious injury were still real dangers – as King Henry VIII found out when he was almost killed during a joust in 1536. Later that same century, however, the popularity of jousting went into rapid decline, as gunpowder made the heavy lancer obsolete on the battlefield and the aristocracy became more interested in high school dressage riding (the training for the light cavalry officer), rather than mounted combat *per se*.

Tournaments became simply mounted games, in which the old training methods replaced the joust itself. Riders tilted at rings suspended from a beam, or at the quintain or Saracen, a dummy and counterweight mounted on a swivelling post. You hit the shield and it swung round, the counterweight dealing you a smart blow across the back unless you ducked immediately. Interestingly, these modified forms of jousting went to the New World along with the early eighteenth-century settlers. In modern Maryland ring jousting is now the state sport. In Europe, however, it seemed that the old way of jousting was dead.

In Scotland in 1839, a group of Ayrshire noblemen, inspired by having read one too many Walter Scott novels, staged the Eglinton tournament, an eccentric, one-off public pageant in which – surprisingly – no one was injured. Perhaps because of the lack of bloodshed, the Victorians failed to revive the sport. Not until well into the following century did jousting really get going again, with the formation of Robert Humphrey's Nottinghamshire Jousting Association at a local riding school in 1970, in response to a tourist board plea for someone to put on some medieval re-enactments at local castles. The resulting shows were wildly successful. Almost overnight, groups of macho-minded horsemen began forming similar clubs all over the UK, a trend that has now spread to the USA, New Zealand and Australia. Full contact jousting, no longer reserved for the nobility, is now controlled by the International Jousting Association, and open to anyone who can ride. It remains, like its medieval predecessor, a highly dangerous sport.

The language of sport
Jonathon Green

Hit for six, kick into touch, throw in the towel, ball-park figure, take a rain check, go to bat, run with the ball, not cricket: sporting imagery is so deeply interwoven into the language that few even give a thought as to whence these everyday phrases emerge. It works on a variety of levels: in the metaphorical foreground come these images that spring from the world of sport; alongside them, practical and specific, are the languages, more properly the jargons, generated by the wide variety of sports on offer. Sometimes the two can blend: the phrase 'bowl a googly', meaning to act in a deceptive manner or ask a difficult question, combines both the essential imagery of a cunning cricket bowler and the ball in question, a googly, an off-break that is delivered with what appears to the batsman as a leg-break action, supposedly invented by the English bowler B J T Bosanquet (1877–1936). But a knowledge of biography is not necessary to use the phrase; indeed, it is most popular in Australia, where the same bowling style is actually known as a 'bosie'.

Sport itself emerges as a word around 1440, meaning a pleasant pastime, an entertainment or amusement, a recreation or diversion. It abbreviates 'disport', itself originally French and meaning, as defined in an early English–French lexicon, 'to play, recreate himselfe, passe away the time'. The underlying Latin – *portare*, to carry – bears the sense of carrying oneself away from things that are more serious and demanding and thus less enjoyable. Sport's linguistic development began barely a century on, in the 1520s, and the word itself quickly adopted two distinct, if complementary, definitions. On the one hand there is sport as sex, meaning 'amorous dalliance' or actual intercourse. Sport as in Kipling's 'flannelled fools' and 'muddied oafs' is a simultaneous arriviste, defined as 'a game, or particular form of pastime, especially one played or carried on in the open air and involving some amount of bodily exercise'.

Of the two, sexy 'sport' (female tennis stars and Linford Christie's celebrated 'lunchbox' notwithstanding) has held up less well. Intercourse has more pungent synonyms on offer now, although the term still persists among older African–Americans. 'Sportsman', a womaniser, is pretty much dead, but its earliest (eighteenth-century) use, in the image of a roistering blade hunting for 'game' in the city's red-light areas, stills bears a sociological, if no longer a linguistic, resonance. The 'sporting house' – or brothel – kept its doors open well into the twentieth century, and the 'sporting gentlemen' – gamblers, but more often pimps – and their sporting women and girls were still to be found within. The sporting life is that of the hedonist, all sex, drugs and rock 'n' roll, not to mention its use as another name for the procurer (thus the character 'Sportin' Life' in the opera *Porgy and Bess*) and indeed his favourite drug, cocaine. With rhyming slang's usual irony, it can also mean one's wife. For Australians 'sporting equipment' still means a condom.

The other sorts of sport – some might suggest the substitute for the more sensual variety – go from strength to strength. As George Orwell pointed out in his essay 'The English People', the British invented most of them and 'the word "football" is mispronounced by scores of millions who have never heard of Shakespeare or Magna Charta'. That was in 1943. Sixty years on and the scores of millions have become hundreds of millions. Yet quantity does not mean quality, and for all its popularity football has failed to create an exceptional vocabulary. 'Sick as a parrot' (the soccer man's take on its seventeenth-century ancestor 'melancholy as a parrot') remains the great football cliché, along with the antithetical, and somewhat more poetic, 'over the moon' (although that too, albeit in a single private letter, existed around 1850). The brief lexicon of football images includes 'play away' (to commit adultery) and 'score between the posts' (which comes from Australian rules football and presumably represents a fusion of the sports fan's ultimate dreams). Does it perhaps say something about sports' respective constituencies that it is the bat and ball games – cricket and especially baseball – that have produced the wordsmiths, typically Ring Lardner and Damon Runyon, whose work as sportswriters would transmute into their lasting contributions to language as whole?

Every sport, like every job and occupation, offers its own jargon. John Eddowes' peerless *Language of Cricket* (1997) runs to more than 500 entries, its pages brimming with 'silly-mid-offs', 'forward-short-legs', 'jaffas', 'mulligrubbers', and 'sticky dogs'. American football's playbooks run to brick-like dimensions, bursting with the arcana, a mix of numbers and letters, that make up each potential variation of the play. Check the internet: aficionados of everything from snooker ('kissing the pink', 'deep screw') to mountain-biking ('banana-scrapers', 'spring planting'), from caving ('brain bucket', 'knobbly dog') to snowboarding ('roast beef air', 'table top'), have their own vocabularies.

Specifics aside, much of our best sporting imagery is a nineteenth-century creation, brought into the language by the contemporary sporting gentry and the boxers, jockeys, trainers and huntsmen with whom they associated. Perhaps the oldest, and in many ways the richest of all, was that which grew up alongside the bare-knuckle prize-fighting of the period. The sporting journalist Pierce Egan, creator among much else of the first ever fictional characters to bear the names Tom and Jerry, published Boxiana, the Fancy's favourite journal. Here one found no blood, only 'claret'; no stomachs, rather 'breadbaskets' and 'victualling offices'; no noses, but 'sneezers' and 'sensitive plants'. Among the many punches or blows are the 'conker' (on the nose), the 'nobber' (on the head), the 'muzzler' (on the mouth) and the 'podger' (to the stomach).

When the Fancy weren't fighting they were at the races, and the track provides another great source of sporting imagery. 'Full of beans' originally referred to a sprightly racehorse; and among others, 'a run for your money', 'turn-up for the book', 'dark horse', 'no-hoper', 'also-ran', 'go the distance', 'neck and neck', and the whole idea of 'form', whether 'good' or 'bad', all spring from the 'sport of kings'. And hunting, another outdoor

'Just not cricket': a streaker stops play at Lord's in 1976

pastime, gives us 'beat about the bush', 'loaded for bear', 'a clean shot', 'come a cropper', and 'sitting duck'.

Sport, with its competitiveness, its winners and losers, its heroes and villains, its dramas and disappointments, is so central to and symbolic of life, it is hardly surprising that its images and terms have crossed the border into the larger vocabulary. It may be no more, to return to Orwell, than war without weapons, but like war with its similar, even bloodier excitements, it has conquered a segment of our language and is unlikely ever to retreat.

The London to Brighton Run
Lord Montagu of Beaulieu

Historians can easily pinpoint the definitive moment when Britain entered the motoring age. It was on Saturday 14 November 1896 when over thirty pioneer motorists set off from London's Metropole Hotel in Northumberland Avenue to drive to the Metropole Hotel in Brighton. The event was organised by the Motor Car Club, an organisation thrown together by its chairman, the rather dubious Henry Lawson.

Great Britain had lagged behind the Continent – both Daimler and Benz built their first cars in Germany in 1886 and France was not far behind – and Lawson was intent on dominating the future of the infant industry by buying as many of the manufacturers' patents as he could. Why it was decided to go from London to Brighton is not recorded, but from Regency days young bloods had ridden horses in relays from London to Brighton and in 1869 the first run for boneshaker bicycles took place on the route.

The November 1896 event was already well organised, with special caps, armlets and oil and petrol available at Reigate. At the start, after a grand breakfast, Lord Winchilsea, the president of the Motor Car Club, warned the competitors – many of whom had had little time to practice – that they were on trial and told them to go carefully. Then he symbolically tore up the red flag, the carrying of which in front of a vehicle had been compulsory until 1873, as three men walking with the vehicle still was. Such was the excitement of the crowds that some cars could not reach the start, including the 1896 Arnold. Today the Arnold is the only running survivor of the original Run and was recently restored by the National Motor Museum.

Of course the presence of horse-drawn traffic was a considerable obstruction and when the cars arrived in Reigate they found it in a state of uproar because of the slow progress, with many cars overheating and breaking down. However, the fact that twenty motorists out of the twenty-two who left Reigate arrived in Brighton without breakdown exceeded even the most sanguine expectations of the organisers. Immediately a squabble took place as to which car got there first, but it is now generally accepted that it was the American, Duryea, who rightly claimed to have arrived at the Metropole at 3.45 p.m.

However, *Autocar* (having printed their current issue in red in celebration) claimed that of the fifty-four cars entered, only thirty-three started, and many had not got far – particularly the electric cars, because of the lack of batteries. Others took the easy way out and transported their cars down by train. Many years later, in 1935, one competitor, Walter Bersey, admitted that his electric car went to Brighton by train, where it was hidden around the corner to wait for other competitors. He even covered it with mud – carefully selected to be the right colour – to make it look as if it had driven on the Brighton roads.

The first revival Run took place in 1927, sponsored by the *Daily Sketch* and the *Sunday Graphic*. From 1930 onwards it was sponsored by the Royal Automobile Club, which has been organising the Run ever since. An important development came after the 1930 Run, when three regular competitors, Sammy Davis, Captain John Wylie and Jackie Masters, drinking together at the Old Ship Hotel, had the idea of forming the Veteran Car Club. The impetus and enthusiasm generated by this new Club enabled many historic cars to be rescued from barns and there were regular Runs up to the Second World War, which naturally curtailed such activities. In spite of severe petrol rationing, the Run started again in 1946 and even then there was an entry of 136 vehicles.

The rules and regulations of the Run have remained unchanged for many years (though the route is quite different from the original Run, because of alterations to the roads – the M23 motorway sensibly bans slow cars). It is still organised by the RAC and only cars built before the end of 1904 are eligible. Only 400 entries are allowed. It is specifically not a race and those arriving too early at Brighton are liable to be disqualified. The only evidence of a successful Run is becoming the proud possessor of a Finisher's Medallion (though members of the Veteran Car Club further enjoy their annual dinner at Brighton.

The London to Brighton Run is by far the most important date in the historic car calendar and attracts commercial sponsorship and entrants from all over the world, particularly America. However, the greatest bolster to the veteran car movement was the 1953 film *Genevieve*, a comedy about the London to Brighton Run, starring Kenneth More, Kay Kendall, John Gregson and Dinah Sheridan. This engendered such enthusiasm that many new Veteran Car Clubs were founded all around the world, and the following year an estimated one million people watched the Run.

My first Run was in 1950 when I took the family 1903 De Dion Bouton with top model Barbara Goalen as my passenger. The car had been on the Beaulieu estate since 1903 and latterly had been used as an estate runabout by the Beaulieu Electric Light Company. For some years it was in store, so unfortunately I had no opportunity of restoring it and it broke down with trembler coil trouble some six miles from the finish. Two years later, it was the very first vehicle to be put on display in the Front Hall of my home, Palace House, in memory of my father, who was a pioneer motorist. Like an acorn, this early display grew into the great tree which has become the National Motor Museum. Over the years, my wife and all the children have completed the Run, cutting their teeth on the sturdy little De Dion Bouton, which is certainly not the easiest car in which to get to Brighton.

My Brighton Runs have always been full of adventures. My slowest was in the De Dion Bouton and my fastest in the 1903 Gordon Bennett racing Napier. My passengers have included HRH Prince Michael of Kent; racing drivers such as Stirling Moss, Graham Hill, Jackie Stewart and Jim Clark; a Miss World; ministers of transport; and

Overleaf: *Taking a short cut during the London to Brighton Run in a scene from* Genevieve, *1953*

even Richard Noble who, a month after breaking the land speed record in Thrust2 at 633.468 mph, completed the Brighton Run safely in my De Dion Bouton. In 1987 my passenger, disc jockey Dave Lee Travis, broadcast his Sunday morning programme live from the seat of the car. However, we were severely overheating and Dave was amazed to be able to tell his listeners that the late Howard Wilson, the Museum's chief engineer, took off his leather trouser belt and made up a new drive belt for the water pump from it! Breaking down is an occupational hazard which we all have to face up to. In 1964, accompanied by Jim Clark, we ran out of petrol at the finish and had to push the car over the line. Jim, having recently been robbed of the World Championship on the last lap, remarked: 'I'm getting used to last-lap dramas.'

Over the years, other historic vehicle clubs have organised their own London to Brighton Runs, starting with the Sunbeam Motorcycle Club in 1930. The Historic Commercial Vehicle Club, of which I am president, held its first in 1962 and the Run now takes place every year in early May.

The London to Brighton Run has an atmosphere all of its own. I know of no other old car event in the world quite like it, and I have been privileged to take part in many. I am sure that the overseas competitors who enter each year would echo my sentiments. You take part whatever the weather – and sometimes it is dreadful. I have known hail, fog or freezing rain, and I have spent many a mile sitting in a puddle of icy water. Sometimes the sun shines and that is a real bonus: rain plays havoc with leather driving belts on the earlier cars and often reduces braking to a gentle rubbing noise. It is the marvellous crowds, though, who really make the event. They line the road from start to finish, just as exposed to the weather as the competitors, but they wave and cheer and every one of them exhorts you to blow your bulb horn! The main problem is the very heavy traffic on the Brighton Road. Modern car drivers do not appreciate the problems associated with driving a veteran. Veterans cannot stop quickly and it is not always possible to give a hand signal – you often need three hands just to drive them! But then I have to agree with Sammy Davis, when he wrote about the same problems in 1936, that they are 'a legitimate hazard of the competition'.

I have hardly missed a Run since 1950, and as the first Sunday of November looms on the horizon the whole of one's life will once again revolve around preparations for this, the longest established and for many of us throughout the world still the most important event in the British motoring calendar.

Lord's Cricket Ground
Peter Hayter

Grace is batting, the sun is out, the pavilion is full. The Prince of Wales, later King Edward VII, holds a smoking cheroot between the fingers of his left hand and on his other arm rests the glove of Princess Alexandra, later Queen, shielding her delicate complexion with a parasol. And there, in the foreground of this painting in the Lord's Museum of an imaginary Test match between England and Australia in 1886, her enquiring gaze directed straight at the eye of the beholder, is the exquisite figure of Lillie Langtry, the Prince's 'special friend'. One simply doesn't know where to look.

And that's the most wonderful thing about Lord's. It's still the greatest place to play cricket and watch cricket and watch the players and watch the watchers in the world.

In recent times the Marylebone Cricket Club – which, though founded in 1787 by sporting members of London's White Conduit Club, played its first match on the present site on 22 June 1814 – has gone purple in its attempts to render headquarters more hip. But while the striking new stands and media centre are spick and span – and floodlights will be next, one fears – such notions seem frankly beside the point of the place. For the fact is that if you want Lord's to be trendy you simply don't get Lord's at all.

Instead, lie back and think of Lord Frederick Beauclerk, a parson, cricket fanatic and inveterate gambler, whose election to the post of MCC President in 1826 was strangely not enough to earn him an obituary in *The Times*, but who made eight centuries here on pitches that by modern standards would be considered unplayable. Think of W G Grace, 'The Champion', after Santa Claus the possessor of the most famous beard in history, waiting growlingly in his yellow-and-red ringed MCC cap and brown leather boots; of Australia's 'Demon' F R Spofforth, with his satanic countenance and black moustaches twitching.

Think of Walter Hammond ordering the ball to the extra-cover boundary with a navy handkerchief emerging from his right hip pocket; of Jack Hobbs, 'The Master', Prince Ranjitsinjhi – 'see the ball, go there, hit it' – or Gilbert Jessop, 'The Croucher'. Think of Charles Fry, who set the world long jump record while at university, played in an FA Cup Final for the Corinthians, represented the Barbarians at rugby and turned down just one challenge in his extraordinary life, namely the offer of the throne of Albania.

Or think of the twenty-one-year-old Donald Bradman, the greatest batsman who ever lived, returning to the pavilion at close of play unbeaten on 155 in his first match at Lord's, the second Ashes Test of 1930, to inform the gateman that it had been 'not a bad bit of practice for tomorrow'.

Think of Denis Compton, the 'Brylcreem Boy', of whom Neville Cardus wrote 'Nature came to him with her cornucopia pretty full, and she let him help himself to it',

Overleaf: *Preserving standards in the Long Room at Lord's: 'Tie!' by Jak*

and the summer of 1947 when he and his pal Bill Edrich both passed the record for the number of runs scored by a batsman in an English season, Compton occasionally arriving at the ground in the dinner jacket in which he had departed the previous evening. Think of Ted Dexter charging down the track to take on the controversial Charlie Griffith in 1963 and score 70 in what many consider the best short innings ever played here.

Think too of Garfield Sobers, whom Wisden called 'the lion of cricket' and whose flair lit up Lord's every time he appeared there; or of Vivian Richards, the 'Masterblaster', and his private duels with his great friend Ian Botham. Think of the youthful Botham overcharging members for their seat cushions during his time on the Lord's ground staff, then scoring 100 and taking 8 for 34 against Pakistan in his first appearance there as a Test player in 1978.

· And let's not forget Michael Angelow, a twenty-four-year-old merchant seaman from St Albans who in 1975 won a £20 bet for streaking across the pitch – 'It's a freaker!' cried John Arlott on *Test Match Special* – only to be advised by the magistrate 'The court will have that £20 … please moderate your behaviour in future'.

Think of Mick Jagger watching from a private box, or his friend Paul Getty whom he introduced to the game in the Sixties. Think of Dickie Bird, in tears on the way out to umpire his final Test at Lord's in 1996, going to the wrong end – he had previously agreed with Darrell Hair that the Australian should take the first over from the pavilion end so that Dickie might avoid being overcome with emotion, but then, presumably overcome with emotion, promptly forgot – but still seeing clearly enough to give Atherton out leg before for nought in favour of India's Javagal Srinath.

Think of the picnickers opening their hampers and popping their corks in the Coronation Garden, or of moments of quiet contemplation in the Harris Memorial Garden; of the Long Room and the feelings all Test debutants experience when they go through it for the first time on their way to the pitch – and of those who come back without scoring, as Gooch did, twice, in 1975.

And think of the sparrow, killed by a ball bowled by Jehangir Khan of Cambridge University to T N Pearce of MCC on 3 July 1936 and immortalised as one of the most famous exhibits in the Lord's Museum – the most famous of all being a bag of ashes and an urn that, no matter how many times Australia beat England at cricket, will remain there until hell freezes over.

And yes, in the time-honoured tradition of such reflective offerings I am prepared to place my name alongside those princes of the game who confirmed, in Jack Bannister's excellent compilation, that 'The Innings of My Life' was played here. Or in my case the ball of my life, sent down chest-high by England's Angus Fraser during a benefit six-a-side tournament on the nursery, that I hit over extra cover for six with my eyes closed (literally). Only one of a thousand reasons why, if I was told I had died and had a choice of heaven, like any sane Englishman or woman I should opt for Lord's, on a velvety-blue-skied Saturday when England are beating Australia in front of a packed house to win the Ashes, over and over and over again.

Frankie Dettori's 'Magnificent Seven'
Robin Oakley

Perhaps once in our lives, if we are lucky, we get to see sporting perfection: Obolensky's try, Jim Laker's ten wickets in an innings, Bob Beamon's leap in the long-jump pit. Mostly, though, it is a matter of individual effort, one man or woman tapped on the shoulder by the gods, totally on song for a day. What made Frankie Dettori's entry into the hall of sporting fame such an achievement is that he had to persuade seven different horses to do it with him on a hotly contested card at Ascot on a single day – 28 September 1996. That was the day that the Italian-born jockey, an honorary CBE and the best showman in British racing for three decades, made sporting history by riding the winners of all seven races on the card, an achievement which probably gave Britain's bookmakers the most painful experience of their lives.

At Ascot that day Dettori, the reigning champion jockey and the best known name in his sport, became a legend. There were early morning prices available from the bookmakers for six of the seven horses he rode. Wall Street could be backed ante-post at 11–4, Diffident at 10–1, Mark of Esteem at 5–2, Decorated Hero at 10–1, Fatefully at 9–2 and Fujiyama Crest at 11–1. The seventh horse was the Ian Balding-trained sprinter Lochsong, who was to come out of the stalls for her race at 5–4. Accepting the starting price for her and the ante-post odds for the others, anybody who took a morning accumulator bet on all seven of Dettori's mounts for the day ahead would have enjoyed odds of 235,834–1 for their money.

The day started with the 2.00 p.m. race, the Cumberland Lodge Stakes over a mile and a half. Dettori was riding Wall Street, trained by Saeed bin Suroor for the Godolphin operation run by the Maktoum family, his main retainers. In Godolphin's familiar blue colours Dettori, despite being up against Paul Cole's proven stayer Salmon Ladder, chose to make all the running, even though his mount, backed down to 2–1 favourite for the race, had not attempted the distance before. The tactics proved right. Dettori was able to steal a look back at the pursuing Salmon Ladder in the straight and, having kept a little petrol in his mount's tank, to hold off his pursuer by half a length.

In the second race, a six-furlong sprint for the Racal Diadem Stakes, Dettori skilfully found a way through, but probably had the crucial piece of luck which forms part of many a sporting triumph. Diffident started at 12–1 after two disappointing runs. But in a slow-run race Dettori coaxed a smooth run from his mount and was flying at the finish, while the favourite Lucayan Prince, ridden by Walter Swinburn, had every kind of traffic problem coming from the rear of the field and just failed to catch him. A stride more and he would have done so. But by then Dettori-backers were sitting on a 39–1 double.

Doubles are fairly commonplace for top jockeys and most punters probably assumed that by then Dettori had used up his ration of luck for the day. But in the third race

Dettori was riding a colt, Mark of Esteem, who had particularly impressed him with his burst of speed on an earlier run at Goodwood, showing a real ability to change gear and quicken up. The Queen Elizabeth II Stakes was an unofficial mile championship of Europe between horses which had won £2 million between them. In the event it turned into a match between the flying filly Bosra Sham, that year's 1,000 Guineas winner, and Mark of Esteem, again trained by Saeed bin Suroor, who had inherited the horse after the falling-out between Sheikh Maktoum and top trainer Henry Cecil. In the final furlong Dettori chose the crucial moment to press the button and Mark of Esteem went away to win by two lengths. Said the jockey: 'The delivery was like a fuel injection – it just knocked me out of my seat.' But again he had timed his effort perfectly against a very good horse. Although he had earlier agreed to a request from course officials not to indulge in one of his famous 'flying dismounts', the showman in Dettori could not resist doing so in the unsaddling enclosure, bringing a roar from the appreciative crowd as he jumped from the saddle.

Now the bookies were starting to hurt and after three winners people were just beginning to ask if this could be Frankie's day in a big way. Money wagered on his mounts in Britain's 9,000 betting shops was being 'blown' back onto the course and could be expected to cramp the odds of what he rode. In the fourth race, a seven-furlong handicap, Frankie was partnering a horse for his long-time ally John Gosden. Though Decorated Hero was carrying a five pound penalty for a recent comeback win after a long lay-off, he was backed down from 12–1 to 7–1. That the odds were no shorter was because the hot favourite High Summer looked like a blot on the handicap. But High Summer, afflicted by a breathing problem, ran poorly and Dettori steered his mount deftly through the field from two out to lead in the final furlong and win by more than three lengths. This time he entered the winners' enclosure with a wide grin and four fingers extended. Suddenly the bookies were beginning to feel a chill and racing journalists were realising they might have a very big story on their hands. The BBC decided to screen more than the four races scheduled.

For the fifth race the appropriately named filly Fatefully, considered likely to start at 5–1 in the morning, was backed down to 7–4 favourite with the seemingly unstoppable Dettori in the plate. This time he had a real race of it. Dettori and Fatefully took the lead a furlong out, but his friend Ray Cochrane, later to rescue Dettori from a blazing Newmarket plane crash and then to retire and become his agent, had other ideas. He gave chase on the 25–1 outsider Abeyr. They closed on him, but Frankie had kept a little in reserve and prevailed by a neck. When after the finish Cochrane called 'Is anybody else getting a chance today?' Frankie yelled back 'No. I'm on fire, mate.'

Journalists by now were feverishly rewriting copy filed for early editions. Leading bookmakers, desperately into damage limitation, were making frantic calls seeking to lay off. And Frankie offered a high five to the crowd as he and his mount walked back into

'I'm on fire': Dettori leaps from Mark of Esteem after the third win of his 'Magnificent Seven'

the now familiar winners' enclosure. There was a *frisson* of alarm among punters when a stewards' inquiry was announced. But although Frankie's mount was held to have interfered with the third, Questonia, the placings remained unaltered.

In the sixth race Dettori was riding Lochsong, due to become a top sprinter for Ian Balding. An interesting betting market developed, with small punters' money in accumulative wagers still flooding in on Dettori and professional punters having some hefty bets on the previously expected favourite Corsini, at more attractive odds than they had expected. The two started as 5–4 co-favourites. Word was that Dettori had been told to drop his mount in behind and come late. Instead he opted to go out in front and make the pace on Lochsong, and although Corsini offered a battle all the way to the line in the hands of Pat Eddery, as the pair pulled five lengths clear of the field it was Dettori again being hailed by a now ecstatic crowd as he equalled the record of six winners in a row held jointly by Alec Russell and Willie Carson. 'A dream,' said Frankie, as he jumped off the horse in the winners' enclosure to applause in which even the officials joined.

Bookmakers now were panicking, laying off where they could the money going on Frankie in the last. Fujiyama Crest, expected in the morning to start at 12–1, was backed down to 2–1 favourite. That he didn't go to odds-on was merely because a number of on-course bookies held their nerve and decided they would take 'mugs' money' at ridiculously low odds for a horse which they reckoned, on the form book, had no chance of winning. Fujiyama Crest had tailed off on his previous run and although he had won the same two-mile race at Ascot a year before, he was set to carry 16lbs more than he had done then.

But they were reckoning without the self-belief of a jockey who was telling his friends 'I am red 'ot' and who was probably capable at that moment of imparting his supreme confidence to anything he rode from the stable cat upwards. Experts can theorise about the debilitating effect of a winner's aura on other competitors. Some writers have wondered whether, in the atmosphere of that extraordinary day, all the other jockeys did their very best to win that last race for themselves. But the simplest answer to that is that, with Frankie going for another all-the-way win, the jockey who came at Dettori's mount through the last furlong on Northern Fleet, and who in the end was beaten by just a neck by the all-out, exhausted Fujiyama Crest, was the hard man Pat Eddery. And they don't come any more competitive than him.

The crowd shouted Dettori home with a collective will for him to win which has probably never before or since been matched on a British racecourse. The bookies had been routed, possibly to the tune of some £30 million. And Dettori completed his 'Magnificent Seven' at cumulative starting-price odds of 25,095–1. It was an extraordinary afternoon's work, showing every facet of race-riding. Dettori exhibited instinctive judgment of pace, coolness in taking swift decisions, enormous strength in the finish, an extraordinary confidence which he communicated to his mounts, and above all an unstoppable will to win. It was an astonishing demonstration of virtuosity and probably the best publicity boost the attention-starved sport of racing had enjoyed in fifty years.

Stanley Matthews: the wizard of dribble
Bobby Charlton

I recently met a man called Ernest Reynolds who was 103 years of age. Born in Salford and an avid Manchester United fan, he had a phenomenal memory, regaling me with stories of clogs, Salford Docks, the First World War and Manchester United of old. Yet sometimes during the conversation he would stop and reflect silently, thinking of the many events he had been witness to during his long life in Lancashire. One such pause was broken when he announced loudly: 'Stanley Matthews! You know, they couldn't get the ball from him. Today's players would stop him, though.' While I agreed with Ernest up to a point, I still thought Matthews would probably find a way.

Sir Stanley Matthews was the first world-renowned footballer, and in the days before television his reputation was known in every country of the globe where football was played. Everyone knew about his dribbling skills, which earned him the nickname 'twinkletoes'. I first saw him with my brother Jack at St James' Park, Newcastle, one Saturday soon after the programme restarted at the end of the Second World War. I must have been about ten and I can still clearly remember the sight of this man we'd all heard about on radio and in the papers. You had to put yourself out a bit in those days to see the Number One in the game.

My brother and I had decided to find a spot in the corner of the ground where we would be close up to the great man. He played for Blackpool then, and even an hour before kick-off at least 50,000 were crammed into St James' to watch him. My first glimpse was when he came out to see what studs they should wear and generally get a feeling of the crowd. He knelt down and tested the pitch with his thumb, deciding whether it would be short or long studs – that was the only choice you had. Then he was out of sight and the next we saw of him was when he came trotting out in the tangerine shirt. Blackpool had many fine players – Farm, Johnson, Mortenson, among others – but all eyes, including mine, were watching only one man that day.

As soon as he got the ball a buzz went round the ground. What would he do? Take on the full-back down his left or his right? It didn't matter to Stanley Matthews. His aim was to cross that dead ball low or high to whoever he thought was best placed to score. Nobody was better at getting past the backs to the line. He had incredible pace, even over a short distance, and would knock the ball past the full-back when he was still six yards away. The poor defender knew that by the time he turned to race with Matthews it was too late: he had gone. His accuracy at crossing the ball was legendary, and Stan Mortenson once told me Matthews even made sure the lace was pointing away from you so it would be more painless to head. I half believe that.

The wizard of the dribble worked hard on his fitness. He didn't drink or smoke and was meticulous with his diet, and at Blackpool every morning he was out on the beach, walking. His father Jack was a boxer and instilled a fitness discipline into Stan that he continued to practise his whole life. He had great speed off the mark, a skill his father also encouraged by getting him to race competitively, even at the age of seven when he needed forty yards' start. But by the time he was fourteen he didn't need any advantage at all. Considering his footwork and pace, you would expect him to have been a regular goal-scorer, but somewhere in his early career I think he realised he was better being a provider and concentrated on that. Bad news, I'm afraid, for poor full-backs who, without help from anyone, were expected to solve the Matthews problem. He demanded the ball to his feet, then turned like a matador towards the defender. Imagine the crowd watching, enthralled. Which way? Left or right? Where now? Where? The ball has gone and so has Stan, and the full-back is on his backside, humiliated. Stan looks up to his forwards. Now, who wants it?

He started his career as a young boy from Hanley in the Potteries, joined Stoke in 1931 and stayed with them right through the war until the 1946–7 season, when he went to Blackpool. This was when he was at his peak and the Matthews legend was born. He was at the Seasiders until 1962, when he was attracted back to Stoke, his home town, for the climax of his life in football. He was fifty years of age, and in his gala match for Stoke the best in the world came to see him play and to pay homage to him.

In the country at large he will be remembered, together with Tom Finney, his great friend and fellow superman of the wing, for the quality of his game and the beauty of his performances. The magic of his personality and his charisma were not lost on me. If anyone attracted me into the game it was Stanley Matthews. He was quite simply a star.

I have seen many full-backs of stature grovelling on the ground, trying to trip him where others have failed. The Cup final in 1953 has been called the Matthews final, because he had never won a cup-winners' medal and the country wanted to cap his great career. The winning goal saw Stan take the play to Barrass, the Bolton Wanderers defender, show him the ball, dip his shoulder to the left, to the right – then look up and pass perfectly to Perry, who had the simplest of jobs finding the net.

Sir Stanley Matthews died in 2000, and his place in football history is assured. At his funeral his coffin was driven round the Stoke City ground and a circuit of the town itself before arriving at the church for the service. The streets everywhere were thronged with people of all ages, many of whom remembered him in the early years. But what impressed me most was all the youngsters, girls and boys, who were respectfully standing, not in silence, but applauding the person they knew had been someone truly unique.

The wizard of dribble: Stanley Matthews shows how he got his nickname, 1956

Stirling Moss' final season
Robert Edwards

1960 had been a truly ghastly year for Stirling Moss. A combination of disasters had hit him in brutally quick succession. His marriage had broken up, he nearly died in a 140-mph crash at Spa, a business venture had gone embarrassingly wrong, and he had even, ironically enough, lost his driving licence. But professionally, as he would prove, he was at the very top of his form.

So he regarded 1961 with some optimism: it was hardly going to be worse than the previous year, whatever happened.

As usual, he drove in a bewildering variety of events, from Formula 2 to the Targa Florio. But it was at the top table, Formula 1, that he proved beyond measure that it was the driver, not the car, which made the vital difference, and in the process confirmed his status as a national hero. Indeed, Moss could by 1961 claim to be the most famous man in Britain, even to those who ignored motor racing.

There was only one Formula 1 car to beat that year and it was a Ferrari, the delectable 156 'sharknose'. Ferrari's Maranello team would lose only two Grands Prix in 1961 and on both occasions it was Stirling Moss who would beat them. Even more extraordinarily, he would do it aboard a privately entered (and prepared) 1960 model Lotus 18 in the Scottish blue colours of Rob Walker. Stirling's association with Walker (whose occupation was listed on his passport as 'Gentleman') went back to 1958, when he had driven what was basically a Formula 2 Cooper to victory in the Argentine Grand Prix. Such an improbable achievement was therefore nothing new, however much it staggered Ferrari and assured Stirling's place in sporting history. To Moss, this was merely what he did for a living.

First blood came at Monaco, when Moss took the lead early and held off the entire works Ferrari team for eighty-seven laps, completing the race at an average within half a second of his pole position time – a place he had earned despite the Lotus having a crack in the chassis, which had been welded together more or less on the starting grid.

At the Nürburgring, a circuit which could hardly have been more different, he took a huge gamble, running the race on disguised wet-weather tyres which were close to disintegration before rain finally arrived. Although he didn't know it at the time, his victory in that race would be his last in a Grand Prix.

That he should have accomplished these wins against what was generally acknowledged to be the finest Grand Prix car on the planet did not go unremarked by its maker, Enzo Ferrari. Moss and Ferrari had not spoken in a decade, their vast collective pride forbidding it. In Stirling's view, Ferrari had treated him badly when he had reneged

The most famous man in Britain: Stirling Moss behind the wheel in his racing heyday

on the promise of a works drive. But ten years later, it was surely time for a truce: 'I need you,' said Ferrari. 'Tell me what kind of car you want and I will build it for you in six months. Put your ideas on paper for me. If you drive for me, you will tell me on Monday what you did not like about the car on Sunday and by Friday it will have been changed to your taste. If you drive for me, I will have no team, just you and a reserve driver. With Moss, I would need no team.'

Heady stuff. But Stirling knew, as Fangio had known before him, that to drive a Ferrari was one thing, to drive *for* Ferrari was something else again. Enzo Ferrari was a Machiavellian man and, as Stirling had learned all those years before, he could not necessarily be relied on. What he declared himself prepared to do to his talented pair of drivers, Phil Hill and Richie Ginther, he might easily do to Stirling himself. A compromise was reached. Ferrari would build a car, but Rob Walker would enter it. It would be a blue Ferrari, something quite unheard of in F1. No privateer had ever entered a contemporary Ferrari Formula 1 car to go head to head with the mighty works team.

Nor, in fact, would they. The deal was kept quiet, but by the opening of the 1962 season, which held even greater promise than the one before, the car was not actually ready. Had it been, the career of Stirling Craufurd Moss might well have developed very differently. For on 23 April 1962, while driving a heavily compromised hybrid Lotus, Stirling had the crash which would end his career as a racing driver. It was his 529th competitive track event and, as so often before, he managed to set fastest lap before disaster struck.

So Enzo Ferrari, having paid the highest compliment a man in his position could give, kept his racing team. He did eventually send a car, while Stirling was in recovery, and a rather puzzled Innes Ireland tried it out. He found it 'interesting but nothing particularly special'.

For in those few months the game had changed irrevocably: motor racing had now firmly become a British sport. The cruel irony – that Britain's greatest exponent of it would never race again – was lost on no one, and it was a thoughtful Graham Hill who won the World Championship that year. But it was Stirling Moss' victories in his final 1961 season, consolidating as they did his spectacular triumphs in the 1958 Grand Prix, that set the seal not only on a glittering racing career but also on Britain's pre-eminence as a motor racing power.

The Old Firm
Graham Spiers

Britain overflows with passion for its football, and perhaps with no wilder exuberance than on the streets of Glasgow. The old Empire's second city has seen its shipbuilding and industrial hearts broken, but one ancient rite from Glasgow's age of heavy industry still refuses to keep quiet. Rangers and Celtic cause a lot of things, including earache. The two great giants of Scottish football, the so-called Old Firm, have been in political ferment in recent years, as has all British football, but their histories and traditions, good or ill, are still bellowed from the terracings.

Historically, the Old Firm regularly drew crowds of 130,000 when they met, a figure which seems mythical today, though even in the modern safety-first age their cathedrals grow ever higher. Celtic Park, a 60,000-seat crater, is filled weekly, and Celtic's supporters intermittently plead with the club to add an extra 20,000. Ibrox, the home of Rangers, holds 51,000, though with 45,000 season-ticket holders the ground is also hopelessly inadequate.

Such passions are built upon more than a century of domination and success. Between them, the Old Firm have won the Scottish Championship a total of eighty-seven times – Rangers with forty-nine titles, Celtic with thirty-eight – and when sixty Scottish Cup successes are also thrown in their hegemony in Scotland is obvious. To add lustre to their lore, European success has also been achieved. Celtic were the first British team to win the European Cup in 1967 and Rangers followed them by winning the former European Cup Winners Cup in 1972.

Belonging to a nation that, in the shadow of England, often expresses an inferiority complex, there is nothing bashful about these two clubs. Celtic's historic winning of the European Cup, with eleven players all born within a thirty-mile radius of Glasgow, prompted Bill Shankly to burst into the winning dressing-room that night in Lisbon and fittingly greet Jock Stein, Celtic's manager, with the words: 'John, you are immortal.' Apart from that majestic triumph, making Celtic's green and white hoops even more famous than they already were, the club needed this victory for no other reason than that they had spent much of the post-war period in the shadow of Rangers.

In one of their booming anthems, the Celtic supporters sing, 'If you know the history ... ', and the history of the Old Firm is beguiling. Celtic were formed by, among others, a priest from the Marist order, Brother Walfrid, who had spent years working among the poor of Glasgow's East End and who had longed for the establishment of a charitable organisation from which the despised Irish immigrant poor would benefit. In forming the Celtic Football and Athletic Club in November 1887, this priest actually

Overleaf: *Mark Viduka of Celtic is tackled by Rangers' Craig Moore, Celtic Park, 8 March 2000*

stated that 'the poor children shall have food and clothing' as a result. It was a founding principle which can be dangerously sentimentalised today, but which nonetheless makes Celtic unique in British football.

Rangers, formed fourteen years earlier, enjoyed less socially painful birthpangs. The club, like many in Scotland in the 1870s and 1880s, came into existence as a direct result of the huge upsurge in feeling and excitement for the great new game of football. On a famous afternoon at the Partick cricket ground in Glasgow in 1872, Scotland played England in the first ever international football match, by which time a host of Scottish football clubs had already been formed.

Given Glasgow's enduring image for its brawny humanity and partaking of the 'bevvy', there is an interesting historic footnote to these times. The same year – 1883 – that the Scottish Football Association was formed, when Rangers and Celtic were in the throes of conception, Glasgow's civic authorities were appalled to note that, within the city itself, a total of 54,446 people had been apprehended for being drunk and disorderly. As one football historian wrote: 'The Scots at that time needed some new form of recreation.' It was thus in part to try to live down this reputation that Rangers and Celtic were born.

The two clubs, like Manchester United, Liverpool, Arsenal and others, have been sucked into the modern age. Given their vast followings, the Old Firm can afford to pay massive wages. In the 1980s Rangers proved the first to break the confines of their Scottishness, persuading players such as Chris Woods and Terry Butcher, the latter the captain of England at the time, to come north and play in Scotland. In the mid-1990s, when first Brian Laudrup and then Paul Gascoigne were imported from Italy, it was a sign that Rangers, like Celtic, were endowed with a prestigious brand name.

Yet the two clubs survive amid inherent social and cultural differences. Celtic, born amid penury, remain more financially circumspect than Rangers. The Ibrox club, with its Protestant roots, and an occasional Protestant superiority syndrome, have been called 'one of the three great pillars of traditional Scottish society', the others being the Church of Scotland and Scotland's unique legal system. Just about every such observation about Rangers and Celtic is open to debate, but the two clubs do unquestionably have distinguishing features which can be traced directly to their past.

The most unfortunate – and often tragic – aspect of their differences is the existence of sectarianism in Scottish society. This sectarianism is itself a complicated consequence of the existence of the Old Firm. Both clubs, to varying degrees, have taken measures to root out their bigoted followers, but any non-Scot arriving to take in the spectacle of an Old Firm match, and alert to the terracing anthems, would have grounds for doubting that any progress had been made at all. In recent years there have even been deaths in the aftermath of these football fixtures. When the two clubs meet, which is at least four times a season, it is the most thorough examination of the mettle of Glasgow's police force.

It is the great contradiction of the Old Firm that they remain at once both one of the tragic and one of the most exciting aspects of Scottish life.

The Oxford and Cambridge Boat Race
Daniel Topolski

As all our best-loved sports fall prey to the lure of the 'professional shilling', one of the last great amateur events has honourably resisted the temptation. Defending that special British bulldog reputation is the Boat Race, a gruelling battle of wills between eighteen unpaid students from Oxford and Cambridge racing in two rowing eights, taking on the elements – and each other – just for the hell of it.

And it's not the low-grade insignificant contest that the tabloid newspapers and a few sniffy feature sportswriters will want you to believe. These are athletes at the peak of their powers, trained to perfection and facing one of the toughest competitions in sport. Many of the contestants, like Matthew Pinsent, go on to win Olympic and World titles. Jonny Searle, Tim Foster, Andrew Lindsay, Luka Grubor, Kieran West, Ed Coode, Ric Dunn, all recent gold medallists, have fought over the winding, treacherous Tideway racetrack from Putney to Mortlake. The courage, conditioning and teamwork honed on the Thames lent them all an extra edge when the time came to take on the rest of the world.

The first races 170 years ago drew great crowds and by the middle of the nineteenth century the banks along the Thames were regularly lined with spectators ten deep for the full four and a quarter miles of the course. Today the nation still divides between dark and light blue – the East End of London traditionally supporting Cambridge an hour up the M11 and the West of the city backing Oxford an hour out along the M4. Over 100,000 fans mass at the start and finish of the race and at the pubs, private houses and bridges along the course. Seven million more watch the live TV coverage (the BBC's fifth-ranked sporting event) and 400 million around the world tune in to the post-race highlights. Calling in at a village chemist in Bali one summer, I caught one of my pre-race interviews, and the long-past Boat Race, on the tiny black and white television set in the corner.

Professional coaches have guided the teams since the late 1980s, financed by sponsorship agreements which began in 1976 when the late Princess Margaret, guest of honour at a fundraising dinner, charmed the chairman of Ladbrokes into supporting the race. Now Aberdeen Asset Management ensures that the event, a massive public operation, is properly presented. But the combatants preparing for the race remain unpaid amateurs, students who come from all over the world, juggling ever tougher college work commitments with the increasingly heavy demands of a full Olympic training programme.

They are for the most part extremely young and inexperienced to be thrust into such a high-profile sporting arena; but they are all utterly dedicated to their singular goal – to win the Boat Race. The clubs they represent only exist for that one race and they know that the result of that twenty-minute explosion of glory will define them for the rest of

Overleaf: *Matthew Pinsent celebrates Oxford's victory in the 1991 Boat Race*

their lives. But they know too that to come second is to be last. Which is why you so often see the losing crewmen collapsed in tears; for defeat was never part of the equation.

Since William Wordsworth's nephew Charles was challenged to a boat race by his Cambridge friend Charles Merivale on 12 March 1829, Cambridge have won seventy-seven times to Oxford's sixty-nine, with one dead heat in 1877. The first race was on the Thames at Henley, but it soon transferred to London, initially between Westminster and Putney. When that stretch became too congested, it was moved upriver in 1856 to run between Putney and Mortlake next to Chiswick Bridge. For the second race in 1836, the Universities chose what were to remain the colours of their racing strips – Oxford opting for dark blue, the colours of their captain's college, Christ Church, and Cambridge adopting Eton College's 'duck-egg' blue. Except during the two world wars, the race has been held annually since 1845.

Fifty years ago training involved a brisk morning walk and a long low-intensity 'paddle' between locks every weekday. The hardest rowing was on race day itself, which sometimes resulted in exhausted, under-prepared oarsmen collapsing well before the finish. Now they row over 5,000 kilometres and train four hours a day during the six-month build-up to the race – that is to say, forty-five hours for every minute of the race – and most will have rowed for four or five years before they even arrive at university. Working close to, and beyond, the edge at full power is a regular part of their weekly programme.

Selection for the final seats in the boat is fierce and pits friend against friend and each man against his own previous performance. Only eight men and a cox make the boat at each university from the original thirty or forty candidates who feel themselves good enough to try; the next eight men make up the Isis and Goldie crews who compete in the 'curtain-raiser' reserves' race half an hour before the main event.

The race has produced much unexpected drama throughout its history, with three mid-race sinkings between 1859 and 1978 for each university, collapsed oarsmen, two mutinies within the Oxford camp – the last, in 1987, immortalised in the feature film *True Blue* – collisions and clashing of oars, assassination threats, and the race halted and restarted by the umpire in 2001.

Boris Rankov, the most successful competitor, won the race six times for Oxford, which also produced the heaviest (17st 5lbs) and lightest (9st 6½lbs) ever oarsmen, the narrowest winning margin (4 feet) and the first woman cox, Sue Brown in 1981. Cambridge hold the record for the tallest man (6ft 9½ins) the tallest and heaviest crew (6ft 6⁹⁄₃₂ins and 14st 13lbs) and the fastest race (16 mins 19 secs). Dry statistics, though, hide the courage, sacrifice and intensity that go into each race and bind together the small band of athletes who have gone the distance. They are as those who have conquered Everest; they share a life-enhancing experience like few others. The imagery that surrounds the event is endearingly old-fashioned: megaphones and coaching bicycles, clashing blades and frozen fingers, schoolboy caps and very tall chaps. But the reality – the quality – springs from the very best of sporting tradition. Which is why the Boat Race will continue to capture the imagination long after rival sporting events have lost their hold on the public mind.

Fred Perry
Virginia Wade

He always reminded me of a cat who had just finished off a bowl of cream. In fact, Fred Perry was quite feline in many ways. For a tall, athletic man, his movements were relaxed and graceful and, above all, ageless. I only knew him way after his prime as an athlete, but he always cut a striking figure and literally purred with good humour.

This was the considerably mellowed version of the stubborn, determined individual who put himself on the map as the greatest British tennis champion. But it was easy to transpose one's impression of him in the present to the days of his prime. He still oozed confidence and would obviously have prowled the court in a magisterial manner. Whenever one saw him, he would come up clutching his perennially unlit pipe, with a big smile on his face and a twinkle in his eye, and would relay either a joke (which was always funny, if not always clean) or an amazingly shrewd comment on a current player. He had an impeccable eye for talent, with a particular liking for the natural player, and was an exceptional analyst of the modern game.

Fred Perry was born in Stockport, near Manchester, on 18 May 1909, the second child of a father who was a trade unionist and eventually an MP. Later the family moved to Ealing in West London, where most of Fred's schooling took place. He was a keen footballer and cricketer, but also a superb table tennis player. Just about everyone played table tennis at home or in social clubs, but not many played like Fred. He was so good that he became World Champion at Budapest in 1929.

But his tennis was not too hot. Tennis players at that time came from a different social stratum from Fred's. It was still predominantly an upper middle-class sport – or recreation, rather – where weekend invitations to private courts and afternoon tea were the custom. The game was at the peak of its popularity, though, with the spectacular French players dominating the winners' circle. In 1922 Wimbledon had moved to its new site in Church Road to accommodate the record crowds flocking to witness such phenomenal players as Suzanne Lenglen and Jean Borotra. Small tennis clubs abounded in the 1930s and there were more than 300 tournaments of stature around the country. It was just such an event that spurred Fred on to his future triumphs.

At the age of fourteen, on a weekend train trip to the coast, he spotted a collection of sleek motor cars near Devonshire Park in Eastbourne. On enquiring of his father as to the owners, the answer came that they belonged to tennis players. Immediately, Fred segued that intelligence into his passport to prestige and escape from the lower classes.

It would be a while before he picked up a tennis racket, but when he did his table tennis expertise stood him in good stead, despite a forehand grip that would make today's coach raise his hourly fee! As a potential road to riches, tennis was a better proposition than ping pong, and his father, influenced by a wise amateur teacher, acquiesced in

supporting him in his pursuit. Fred was given a year to prove himself. It was a year in which, with the help of a coach, he applied his innate tactical savvy and his desire to conquer the game. This was no Nick Bollettieri camp – not total immersion with an endless supply of players as sparring partners, hitting hours of balls with stroke, psychology or fitness specialists. This was just Fred with his self-belief, determined to find the winning formula to his forehand. He did just that. He hit the ball early on the rise as a running forehand, as an approach shot, as an inside-out winner or as a volley. He dominated the court with it. His limbs were long and rangy and those legs could move to protect his somewhat defensive backhand. As for his serve, his action was perfect. As a young, eager teenager without a coach, I asked Fred to help me with my serve. To this day I can remember his advice: 'Let the racket drop like a pendulum.' In thirty minutes he had given me a blueprint for a lethal weapon...

Along with his gritty northern character, he had plenty of motivation to harpoon success as an entrée into the world of respect and status that was otherwise cordoned off from him. I don't believe he cared about acceptance, but he wanted the power to say 'Take notice of me'. With his table tennis prowess he already had the taste of winning – and once you have experienced that, you are not satisfied with anything less. He was young enough to feel he could conquer the world: with his ability and his bravado, fame was just waiting to happen. Imagine what that package would portend today. His extrovert personality, twinned with his dynamic looks and bearing, would have agents and media swarming around him like seagulls following the new catch. But more than that, he would have been guaranteed millions of pounds in endorsements, even before he won a single event.

Not that there was ever any worry about winning. In no time he was showing results. These successes propelled him into the 1931 Great Britain Davis Cup team. A young, inexperienced team – Perry, Bunny Austin and Pat Hughes – they did brilliantly to reach the finals, where they lost to those magnificent French musketeers. It only took them two more years to wrest victory from the French when, playing in front of the unrestrainedly partisan crowd at Roland Garros, they brought the Davis Cup back to Great Britain after twenty-one years. They had beaten the United States in the semi-final and France in the final, Fred winning the final match and achieving the best individual record for a season.

Fred was a dedicated worker, spending hours practising with the help of Dan Maskell, the All England Lawn Tennis Club and Davis Cup coach. After losing a long five-set match, he vowed to make himself the fittest man in tennis and thereafter, alongside his hard work on court, he also joined in with the rigorous training sessions of the Arsenal football team. The recipe worked. Later that year, 1933, he won his first Grand Slam title at Forest Hills, defeating the great Australian Jack Crawford in the final. Jack was an immensely popular, laid-back, personable player, but he could not quite control the nervous pressure of holding the previous three Grand Slam events and he succumbed to Fred's tenacity and extra fitness. This was just the beginning for Fred. The following year he again triumphed over Gentleman Jack in the Australian Open, then went on to stun him in three straight sets in the Wimbledon final. Despite the fact that he was the first British champion in twenty-five years, his brashness disenchanted some of the straight-laced officials of the AELTC. The new champion would customarily be congratulated and given his new club tie, but while Fred was in the bathroom after his win, he overheard the official telling Crawford that the wrong man won before just leaving the tie on the back of Fred's chair.

Feline grace: Fred Perry leaps to return a ball at Wimbledon in June 1936

A thin skin was not part of Fred's make-up. He specialised in needling opponents, but as one of his long-time friends and fellow competitors, Sydney Wood, told me, 'Fred was the player the others most liked to hate. Off the court he would make remarks like "I'm glad I'm not playing me today, I feel so good". Or he would boast that he was better trained athletically than his adversaries. But on the court he was totally straight and fair, and he became a wonderful, giving guy.'

He added two more Wimbledons to his tally of titles, beating Baron Gottfried von Cramm, a player of immense talent whose career was mutilated by the Third Reich, whom he dared to criticise. Fred was a member of all Great Britain's four Davis Cup-winning teams. He also won the French Championship in 1935 – beating Crawford and von Cramm – and a total of three US Opens. He was one of only five players to win four consecutive Grand Slam tournaments, though since they didn't lie in one calendar year they didn't make him a Grand Slam winner, a feat only accomplished by Don Budge and (twice) by Rod Laver.

Public adoration and huge success had given Fred all the fame he desired, but it didn't bring him wealth or a happy relationship with the tennis bureaucracy, which then as now contained its inflexible elements. So it was perhaps not surprising that at the end of 1936 Fred accepted an offer from Bill Tilden to join his professional circuit in the US, where instead of the twenty-pound vouchers that accompanied his golden trophies he would earn good money (and use his name to endorse a clothing line). He had ample success on the well-attended pro tour, spent more time in the US with his actress wife Bobby and, fed up with the disgraceful way he was treated by the LTA, decided to become a US citizen. Needless to say, there was a huge amount of resentment that he had forsaken defence of his Wimbledon crown and the Davis Cup, leaving Great Britain so mortally weakened in tennis talent that to this day they have never recovered.

For many years he was pretty much *persona non grata* in the UK. Eventually, a more enlightened hierarchy would take over, modern enough to appreciate Fred and his extraordinary accomplishments, and he and Bobby became central to the British tennis scene. The BBC had the foresight to ask him to be a radio commentator, in which capacity, right up to his death, he entertainingly educated the public about the game he understood so well. The top players all had a respectful regard for him as a champion and a generous human being confident enough in his own achievements not to begrudge anyone their success and huge monetary rewards. If Tim Henman had won Wimbledon while Fred was alive, Fred would have been the first to congratulate him.

Fred Perry continues to garner posthumous fame as the years go by without another British men's player becoming Champion. When he passed away in 1995, at the Australian Open, the LTA had the inspiration to organise a memorial service at St Paul's Cathedral prior to Wimbledon. It was a stirring occasion – and as, together with Pete Sampras, Martina Navratilova and John Newcombe, I read a verse of Kipling's 'If –', you could almost hear Fred chuckling from above at the ironically splendid send-off.

The Queensberry Rules
Henry Cooper

The rules of the London Prize Ring, originally drawn up in 1743 and revised in 1838, had produced in Prize fighting a sport that had, by the 1860s, become pretty unacceptable. It was dangerous, uncivilised and frankly cruel. As a result, it was more or less driven underground: bouts would take place only on private property, as public matches were all too often illegal. Boxing was really turning into a latter-day equivalent of bear baiting and – given the fact that mid-Victorian England was quite a politically correct place, at least on the surface – would probably have been consigned to history in just the same way.

The Queensberry Rules changed all that.

The Marquess of Queensberry did not write them himself – the author was actually a man called John Graham Chambers. Chambers was a keen member of the Amateur Athletic Club, an organisation which later gave rise to the Amateur Boxing Association, and like many people he wanted to see proper pugilism – as opposed to the gruesome free-for-all that boxing had become – develop as an independent sport. He is often confused with a professional middleweight of the same name, Arthur Chambers, who was also a friend of Queensberry and did indeed spend time with the Marquess promoting the new rules, particularly in America, where the two went on tour together; but while Arthur clearly had a role to play, and may have been consulted about the rules, it was John who was their real begetter.

John Chambers' new rules were written in 1864–5 and published two years later, but it was the support and sponsorship given by the sporting 8th Marquess of Queensberry (famously also the catalyst for the libel trial that consigned Oscar Wilde to Reading Gaol) which resulted in their being adopted by the AAC. The first fight under the new rules took place in 1872, and quite quickly people saw that boxing (as opposed to merely fighting) was now a sport in its own right.

The most important article was the second: No wrestling allowed. This meant that the science of boxing could now develop as a discipline quite separate from the old Prize Ring. To put it another way, wrestlers were no longer allowed to punch. Also important was Article 8, which made boxing gloves compulsory. Most bizarre to our eyes was Article 10, banning the use of springs in boxers' boots, which suggests that some enterprising fellow had at least given that a try!

Of course, professional bare-knuckle fights still went on (and indeed still do today), but the official sport was now evolving in a way that a modern audience would recognise, with three-minute rounds, a minute interval between each round, and so forth. Importantly, boxing now depended as much upon skill as it previously had upon brute strength.

The new rules saved men from a huge amount of physical punishment, which is what they were written to do. It was always going to be difficult to persuade amateurs to take part in the old sport, where men fought almost until they dropped. The gradual adoption of the Queensberry Rules edged out the old eighteenth-century regulations (such as they were) and totally re-invented the sport.

At the time, many people thought the new rules were unmanly, and I'm told there was a degree of resistance to them among the real diehards who fought for money. My grandfather George was a keen middleweight fighter and boxed bare-knuckled as well as with gloves on. Sadly, he died before I was born, so I never had the chance to ask him which rules he preferred. I do know this, though: Grandpa would cheerfully fight a twenty-round bare-knuckle bout in a pub stable-yard after church on Sunday and win half a sovereign, but by the time he arrived home his hands were so stiff and swollen that he couldn't even take the money out of his trouser pocket; my father had to do it for him. Those were cheap days – the family could live quite well for a week on his winnings – but they were bleak ones indeed.

Almost all the later rules that came in were refinements of the Queensberry approach, trying to make the sport as safe and civilised as possible without losing its essential danger and spectacle. No physical contact sport can ever be 100 per cent safe of course, but the important effect which the rules had was to open boxing up. No one in their right mind, and certainly no sensible amateur, would have dared climb into a ring with some of those early Prize-fighters (although I remember a couple of my opponents who might well have had a go!), but once there were rules which made sense to everyone it was a different matter, and boxing became hugely popular when it emerged back above ground once more.

The first world heavyweight champion under the Queensberry Rules was John L Sullivan, and just to show that it was still not all plain sailing, his first serious title defence lasted seventy-five rounds before his opponent's handlers finally threw in the towel.

So the Rules built a sporting model which saved lives, and it is no exaggeration to say that they probably saved the sport as well. Without them, I doubt very much that the sport I came to love would have developed at all. I didn't realise it at the time (I was a bit distracted), but when I retired in 1971 almost exactly a century had elapsed since the first bout had been fought under the Chambers/Queensberry Rules. In one sense everything had changed by then, but in another it was still essentially and recognisably the same game. I have every reason to be grateful to Mr Chambers and the Marquess.

Gloves off: Welsh boxer Jim Driscoll in 1910

Steve Redgrave's Gold Medals
Simon Barnes

Steve Redgrave is not the greatest athlete in this book. Rather, he is every single one of them. Every great sporting achiever featured in these pages is Steve Redgrave: in fact, every high sporting achiever that ever played a ball, sat on a horse, lifted a weight, somersaulted, grappled, pirouetted, threw a punch, dived into the water or sat on top of it is, at base, Steve Redgrave.

We might define Redgrave as the difference between being very good at sport and being a champion. Or, if you prefer, the difference between being a champion and being a great champion, a serial champion, a champion of champions.

One way that potential champions locate the Redgrave within is by the manner in which they practice. Daley Thompson said that his rivals in the decathlon never trained on Christmas Day, so he always did. And to ram the point home – the point being superiority to everybody else on the planet – he did so not once but twice. Redgrave's sporting life was an eternal round of self-sacrificing, self-glorifying training: training in great quantity but, more importantly, of relentlessly high quality. Training miles strengthen the body: but the knowledge that you have trained more often and better than everyone else germinates a tiny seed of contempt for people who try less hard, who want it that little bit less.

But above all, you locate the Redgrave within at the final stage of the contest: and that is true whether you are throwing a dart at the double, making the double-layout dismount from the high bar or facing a double-fault as you serve at match-point down. Someone once asked Pete Sampras what was going through his mind at just such a crisis in the final of a major championship. After a pause he gave the perfect answer: 'There was nothing going through my mind at the time.'

There is a Zen-like purity in this: and Zen is something that takes you beyond yourself, beyond the limitations you see for yourself. Redgrave has this ability in superplus. We are used to the notion that sport does not build character: rather, it reveals character. But Redgrave remains fearsomely enigmatic. You can't say what it is about him. He eludes analysis. He has never fitted into the merry soap opera of sport: he is not a Michael Schumacher, a David Beckham, a Venus Williams. He has neither the right sport nor the right temperament to be a 'character'. He stands instead for a kind of monolithic victoriousness: a hero, flawed and human all right, but beyond our reach, beyond easy understanding.

Journalists always felt compelled to call Redgrave 'an Olympian'. This is an unusual choice of word: it is not often used even for people who have had conspicuous success in the Olympic Games. It does not suggest that Redgrave has something of the gods about him: gods win without effort. No: Redgrave is Olympian in the manner of the mountain.

He has a quality of massiveness that is only partly to do with physical stature.

Yet Redgrave did not win public affection until the very end. He had that unsympathetic quality of pure self-certainty. This is not something you meet very often; and the sport of rowing is not one in which personalities shine out. Redgrave was not a man of many words; aware of his lack of ease with them, and perhaps realising that his brooding, mountainous qualities told us more than any assurance that he was taking each race as it came.

He won his first Gold Medal in the four in 1984, and then won in a pair with Andy Holmes. After their divorce, he won Gold for a third time with Matthew Pinsent. This was one of the big relationships of Redgrave's life: Redgrave, a comprehensive schoolboy, found himself living in terms of close intimacy with this teasing, self-confident, drawling Old Etonian.

It was a match made in heaven. It gave an altogether unexpected touch of humour and lightness to Redgrave's attitude – something which I am certain made it possible for him to continue beyond his own expectations – and it gave to Pinsent even more of the quality he already had, the quality we have for convenience called Redgrave.

There is a story about the year in which they won their second Olympic Gold Medal together. There was a rumour that they had had training setbacks, they were faltering, they were there for the taking. The crews lined up for the first big final of the Olympic year, dreaming that they could take over from the surly Englishman and his grinning mate. As they came forward on their slides in readiness for the first stroke, Redgrave growled into Pinsent's ear: 'Let's crush some dreams.'

And so the fourth book of the epic was written. But it was the fifth and final book of the Redgraviad that made Redgrave loved; for it was the one that showed his weaknesses. At the last, it was his weakness that made his strength vivid. After winning that fourth Gold, Redgrave had melodramatically announced his retirement with the words: 'Anyone who sees me in a boat again has full permission to shoot me.'

It was perhaps inevitable, then, that he came back for just four more years of hell. This time he set out to do it in a four, because he was feeling the hammering of the years. Then he went down with diabetes, a disorder which can wreck the lives even of those who live without physical stress. His crew were heavily beaten in one of the Olympic prep-races: the dream-crusher's own last dream was well stomped on.

So it was in an atmosphere of fear and doubt and uncertainty that the final race took place, in Sydney in 2000. I was there, and I thought they had been caught at the line. But even as I groaned in disappointment, I heard wild cheering and learned the truth of it. They had held on to win by the width of a fag-paper or two. When did you think you would win, Steve? 'It was never in any doubt after 250 metres.'

Which was a wonderful Redgravian line to put at the end of Book Five. Redgrave: the man who won. When anyone else wins, Redgrave should get royalties.

Overleaf: *The Olympian: Steve Redgrave with the fifth of his five Gold Medals, Sydney, 2000*

Red Rum
Stephen Moss

Have you ever been on the course or even in a bookie's when one of the great steeplechases begins? The roar of anticipation, the sighs when one of the favourites falls, the frenzy of the last quarter-mile? These great races – the Cheltenham Gold Cup, the King George, the Whitbread, the Hennessy – last three miles or more, long enough for a complex story to unfold, for a horse to demonstrate skill, tenacity and courage, for a race to be won and lost half a dozen times. And then, standing alone, there is the Grand National (the 'Grand' is superfluous; 'the National' is enough the world over): four and a half miles, thirty frightening fences, up to forty brave horses, a large crowd to will them on, a vast audience of once-a-year punters shouting the odds.

We have had some great steeplechasing heroes: Golden Miller, winner of five Cheltenham Gold Cups as well as the National in 1934; Arkle, winner of three successive Gold Cups; Desert Orchid, a striking grey horse adored by the public and winner of four King Georges and a Gold Cup. Golden Miller and Arkle were supreme performers; 'Dessie' a people's champion. But one horse managed both to set a new standard and to capture the heart of a nation. The horse was Red Rum, and he did it because his domain was Aintree, the Liverpool home of the National since 1836.

Red Rum is the only horse to have won the National three times – in 1973, 1974 and 1977. Six horses had won it twice before Red Rum, but the double had not been achieved since Reynoldstown in 1935–6. Even the great Golden Miller won only once in five attempts; Arkle never confronted the Aintree monster. To win back-to-back Nationals in 1973–4 was remarkable; to come back in 1977 at the age of twelve and win again was little short of miraculous. In between those triumphs, Red Rum had been second in 1975, giving 11lb to the brilliant L'Escargot, and second again in 1976, giving 12lb to Rag Trade. The main reason that multiple winners of the National are rare is not that, having won once, they anxiously come back knowing Becher's Brook has to be jumped twice. It is that once a horse wins, it is thenceforth less favourably weighted. Red Rum was always top weight after his win in 1973.

Red Rum hailed from a stud in Ireland and there was little in his background to suggest that he was a legend in the making. His mother (or dam, in racing parlance) was too temperamental to be any good on the racecourse, his sire noted chiefly for his speed in sprints. Four and a half miles would have been unthinkable for either, and the two-year-old 'Rummie' made his debut in a low-grade flat race over five furlongs. The runes, though, were there to be read: amazingly, that first race was at Liverpool and he dead-heated with a horse called Curlicue. Not that anyone was reading them just yet: Red Rum

Red Rum shows his mettle in 1973, the year of the first of his three Grand National wins

passed through several sets of hands, had four different trainers and in his ten-year career was ridden by no fewer than twenty-four jockeys, including Lester Piggott. His flat career was exactly that – flat. But all that changed when in August 1972 he was bought by the wealthy octogenarian Noel Le Mare, who had set his heart on winning the National, and was placed in the hands of Donald (aka 'Ginger') McCain, a former taxi-driver who ran a small stables at the back of a second-hand car dealer's showroom in Southport.

In flat racing, the great prizes usually go to multi-million-pound operations and trainers with large complexes at Newmarket. In jump racing, everything is scaled down. Any owner can get a realistic shot at the major races, and the only complex McCain had before he happened on Red Rum was about how to pay the bills every month. Flat racing is science: breeding plus money equals success. Jump racing is art: poetry in motion. Red

Rum was an average flat horse with dodgy feet (he had been diagnosed as having a progressive bone disease called pedal ostitis), but something remarkable occurred when McCain took on the seven-year-old and started exercising him on the sands at Southport. The sea did wonders for his feet and in his first season with McCain he won six of his nine races, culminating in his first National.

Curiously, Red Rum was the villain of that race, getting up in the closing strides to beat the bold, front-running Crisp, who was conceding almost two stone to his rival. There are many contenders for 'greatest National', but that 1973 epic, with Red Rum making up twenty lengths on the run-in, is one of the unquestionable classics. Villain turned hero when he saw off Gold Cup winner L'Escargot in 1974 and followed that with those brave, top-weighted seconds. Then came 1977, when the only real threats were from two loose horses running alongside him and from an ecstatic crowd spilling onto the course as he approached the finishing line. Brian Fletcher, who had ridden Red Rum to his first two National successes, had given way to the Irishman Tommy Stack by 1977. Stack, in tears as he was led to the winner's enclosure, said the horse gave its jockey an enormous feeling of confidence, seeming to say 'this is my place, this is my race'.

When Rummie won his first National in 1973, ownership of the course was about to change hands and the very survival of the event was in doubt; when he won his third in 1977 (he was entered for the next three but, perhaps thankfully, injury kept him out), its future was almost secure. The National had made Red Rum; and he in turn did his bit in re-establishing the National.

That record-breaking third victory is now a generation away. Over time, memories fade: Golden Miller is a name known now only to the racing cognoscenti. A recitation of races won cannot capture the essence of a great horse; that resides in the hearts of those who witnessed his deeds. The sportswriter Hugh McIlvanney saw each of Red Rum's assaults on the Everest of steeplechasing and, in an article written a year after his third Aintree victory, explained what the horse meant: 'In animal-loving Britain, no animal has ever been loved like this one. His hold on the affections of the nation utterly transcends racing. Schoolboys and grandmothers, turf aficionados and once-a-year 50-pence punters cherish him for reasons more compelling than his brilliance. They love him because he is a classic hero figure, because he rose from the harshest of working-class backgrounds and travelled the stoniest of roads to stardom, and because he made it on his ability, his smartness, his resilience, and most of all on the burning purity of his spirit.'

Rummie died in 1995 aged thirty, veteran of five Nationals and several thousand supermarket openings (he also turned on the Blackpool illuminations and was a star turn at the Sports Personality of the Year Awards; had it been open to quadrupeds, he would undoubtedly have won). It is said that he received more obituary column inches than Kingsley Amis and Alec Douglas-Home: what are novelists and prime ministers compared with a once-in-a-lifetime racehorse? Red Rum is buried at Aintree with his proud head facing the winning post, as if still ready to fly past it and accept the applause of a doting crowd.

The Ryder Cup
Ian Botham

Cricket was my profession and my professional life. I never did a thing on the field I regretted. (Off it, don't ask.) But whereas perhaps I was and am too closely involved in the sport ever to have been able to lie back and enjoy it for pure pleasure, golf, along with fishing, will always be my real sporting love affair. I've been lucky and privileged to have played with some of the real stars of the British game, like Nick Faldo, Sam Torrance and my little but great friend Ian Woosnam, and it is never a surprise to me that whenever two or more of us are together in one place the subject very nearly closest to our thoughts is the Ryder Cup.

To locate the standing of the Cup in the global sporting league requires little more research than a glance at television viewing figures. With the 2003 battle between the best golfers of Europe and the United States at the Belfry set to be beamed into more than half a billion homes around the world, only soccer's World Cup and recent Olympics can lay claim to more armchair fans. Golf's fiercely contested biannual Transatlantic challenge is now right up there in its ability to provide nail-biting action and is a classic case of the tiny acorn that grew into a magnificent oak.

For it was Samuel Ryder, a market gardener from St Albans, who used part of the fortune he made from selling seeds in one-penny packets to commission jewellers to create the gold trophy that is now the object of such fierce intercontinental rivalry. Were he alive today, Ryder would probably disapprove of the event which still bears his name. When he took a group of eight British club professionals to the Worcester Country Club in Massachusetts in 1927 his aim was to foster friendship with their American counterparts, and just as important as the golf was the sport of consuming an excellent dinner and fine wines. A man after my own heart.

The Ryder Cup retained that low-key tradition for fifty years, mainly because the Americans won so often that it could barely be considered an even contest. Indeed, British journalists attending the 1975 Ryder Cup at Laurel Valley, Pennsylvania, recall that they almost outnumbered the spectators lining the fairways. In 1979, officialdom stepped in to try and level the playing field and raise interest when the Great Britain team was expanded to take in the best players from continental Europe, giving the 22-year-old Seve Ballesteros his first taste of the Ryder Cup. Europe still managed to lose the next three contests but it was the dashing Spaniard, with the magical short game which could rescue so many seemingly lost causes around the greens, who changed the face of the Ryder Cup forever.

During the final afternoon singles in 1983 at the PGA National course in Palm Beach, Florida, Ballesteros, who had found a bunker off the tee at the final hole, produced a memorable three-wood recovery shot against Fuzzy Zoeller that was to earn a precious half-point for Europe. Ballesteros' team lost that match by the smallest of margins –

13$\frac{1}{2}$ to 14$\frac{1}{2}$ – but it was in the locker room afterwards that the Spaniard played the masterstroke that was to change the face of the Ryder Cup forever. As his teammates sat silent, exhausted and forlorn, Ballesteros issued a rallying cry. To get so close was not failure, he said, but the final proof that the gap between the States and Europe had become so close that victory would be there for the taking next time.

And how right Seve turned out to be. When the teams lined up at the Belfry two years later, Tony Jacklin, Europe's non-playing captain, had at his elbow a quartet of players that was to pocket a host of the world's major golfing titles in the Eighties. There was Nick Faldo, the ice-cool Englishman with the immaculate robotic swing; Sandy Lyle, the

Scot and that year's Open Champion, whose almost permanent smile concealed a steely determination; Bernhard Langer, the toughest of matchplay competitors and the finest golfer ever produced by Germany – and there was Ballesteros himself, two years older and by then the most exciting golfer in the world.

Palm Beach had stoked up an appetite for the Ryder Cup among golf fans for the first time and although the two teams went into the final day's singles at the Belfry with Europe marginally ahead, none of their supporters dared think that the US's superiority would finally be broken. But Sunday's early singles matches turned out to be a glorious procession as Manuel Pinero, Paul Way, Lyle and Langer all produced priceless points, and the moment when Sam Torrance played his vital long putt over two different curving layers of the eighteenth green to clinch victory against Andy North, and Europe's first Ryder Cup win for 28 years, produced tears, hangovers and memories for millions.

Ever since then, every shot in the Ryder Cup has become a worldwide event, played under intense pressure and scrutiny. At times the rivalry between the two professional tours of the United States and Europe has exceeded the bounds of acceptable behaviour as laid down by golf's great sporting tradition – and anyone sniggering at me talking about acceptable behaviour will report to my study after class – but amidst the joys of victory and the despair of defeat there have also been moments of great sportsmanship. At Valderamma in 1997, Europe's Colin Montgomerie threaded through the trees the drive of his life for the half-point he needed to clinch the Ryder Cup for Europe. Having achieved that goal, he conceded a 20-foot putt to his opponent Scott Hoch, ensuring their particular match ended all square rather than with the American bearing the burden of losing the whole point for his beaten team.

Over the years, the Ryder Cup has produced many unforgettable shots, but one above all encompasses the coolness of mind that is required when the pressure reaches boiling point. It was the third shot played by Nick Faldo at Oak Hill Country Club in 1995 when Europe, having lost the Ryder Cup the previous year, were in danger of failing again. At one stage Nick had been three holes down with three to play against Curtis Strange, but had fought his way back to just one down standing on the eighteenth tee, knowing that victory at the hole would earn half a point and clinch the match. When his drive found semi-rough on the right-hand side of the fairway Faldo could have gambled everything by attempting to fire his recovery shot straight at the flag. Instead he played a short iron back onto the fairway, fired a wedge in to three feet from 110 yards out and sank the putt.

It is a sequence of shots we have relived time and again during our long and unending pursuit of the perfect Rioja moment. And despite the many setbacks we have endured, we do not intend to stop now. As a sportsman looking at other sportsmen, I can often feel what it must be like to be in the spikes of those guys. As a punter loving the sheer spectacle of it, I am as wrapped up in the fantasy of it all as the next man. I know which feeling I prefer.

Tony Jacklin, team captain, holds onto the Ryder Cup for Europe at the Belfry in 1989

Britain's world land and water speed records
Richard Noble

The buccaneering spirit of land speed record racing has always appealed to the British. There is a compulsive attraction in the glory of being the very fastest ever, not to mention the mix of speed, power, risk, courage and advanced engineering – the power requirement for a speed record vehicle increases as the cube of the speed: go twice as fast and you need eight times the power. The established rules are deliberately few in order to encourage ultimate design: basically, four wheels or more, a driver who really controls the monster, and two passes in opposite directions over the measured mile or kilometre within sixty minutes.

The first formal race for the world land speed record took place shortly after the first cars appeared. In 1898 Count Chasseloup-Laubat achieved the magic speed of 39 mph on the Achères Road near Paris – not quite as fast as the bicycle record at that time, but nevertheless the first ever land speed record. The British first wrested the record from the French in 1924 and were to see it right through to the sound barrier in 1997.

In the 1930s the land speed record racers were treated as national heroes. They were risk-takers, with early technology and very limited means of performance and safety prediction. Best known was Sir Malcolm Campbell, who between 1924 and 1935 made a highly successful career of raising the record from 146 to 302 mph. His obsession soon outgrew not only the available engines but also the available geography. His first record was taken at Pendine Sands, Wales. Later he ran out of space at Daytona Beach in Florida. In the end he found the famous Bonneville Salt Flats in Utah, where the salt gave tyres far greater grip and cooled them at high speed. It also provided the hard, smooth surface of an ice rink, enabling errant cars to dissipate speed and energy in long, safe slides.

A hardy Scot, Sir Malcolm became hooked on speed while racing at Brooklands, financing his LSR cars from corporate sponsorship and wealthy friends. He effectively ran a land speed record business – developing his Bluebird car with a small team and profiting from the publicity and endorsements generated by an explosively growing motor industry. Year after year Campbell and his car broke records; he survived near-fatal experiences and the legend grew. But in 1935, while shooting at the magic 300 mph mark in his now 2,500 hp five-tonne car, a front tyre burst at 304 mph. Sir Malcolm fought the car to a halt and was faced with a life or death dilemma. The first run was timed, but the car had clearly outrun the tyre technology; another failure could mean death. There was no point in returning slowly – so he took a deep breath and raced back through the mile, hoping the fresh tyres would hold. They did, and after a timekeeping error the new record was announced at 301 mph, the first over 300 mph. Sir Malcolm, now nine times land speed record holder, decided this was a sensible point at which to exit and subsequently devoted his energies to the water speed record instead.

Not so much is known about John Cobb, the man who broke the 400 mph land speed barrier. Cobb was the record-breaker's record-breaker. Unlike Campbell, he appears to have had little interest in publicity; by all accounts he was a man so quiet that it was difficult to obtain an interview, but one who was obsessed with, and above all enjoyed, speed. Cobb graduated at Brooklands, achieving the incredible outer circuit record of 143 mph in 1935, a record which stands in perpetuity. To put this in perspective, imagine driving a 1930s car with the basic suspension of a lorry around steeply banked rough concrete at 160 mph. Cobb teamed up with Reid Railton, the designer/modifier of the last Bluebird, who created an incredibly advanced integrated design: the Railton Mobil Special, featuring four-wheel drive and the most aerodynamically advanced racecar body ever seen. Cobb was very much a team man, delegating control of the programme to the builder Ken Taylor and taking orders as the driver. In 1939 Cobb and the Railton raised the record to 369 mph and in 1947 to an incredible 394 mph. On the second run Cobb, sitting ahead of the vast mass of engines and drive-trains in light cotton overalls and without a crash helmet, drove the Railton to a one-way speed of 403 mph. So great was the achievement that the wheel-driven land speed record has only advanced 50 mph in more than fifty years! John Cobb was to die tragically at Loch Ness in 1952 when his jet boat Crusader broke up at 240 mph.

As Sir Malcolm's son, Donald Campbell had a tough act to follow. He chose to specialise in the water speed record, which had the advantage that it could be attempted in Britain, but the disadvantage that it didn't attract the interest, technology and support of the vast motor industry. Development technology was limited to wind tunnels and water tanks, and the jet-powered Bluebird boat had to be developed by highly risky trial and error. Whereas the LSR cars had a hard running surface and relatively predictable aerodynamics, a water speed record boat runs on a compliant and variable surface. Speed record vehicles tend to be divergent in pitch, meaning that if the car or boat were to pitch up beyond a small angle there would be insufficient opposing aerodynamic force to counter the pitch and the vehicle would fly.

Donald Campbell was a great showman, much loved by his team for his determination and sense of humour. Like his father, he mixed publicity with performance, gradually raising the water speed record every year – from 1955, when he broke the 200 mph barrier with a 202.32 mph record on Ullswater, to 1964, when he clocked up 276.33 mph in Australia – and generating a high level of awareness both on and off the water. The water records were not easily achieved – the small team worked in basic conditions, undertaking major design modifications by the freezing waterside at Coniston in the Lake District – and in 1960 Campbell switched his attention to the land speed record, achieving, despite an appalling crash at Bonneville in 1962, a new 403 mph record in Australia in 1964. Already, however, the Americans had discovered the greater potential of jet-powered cars. By 1965 Campbell's record had been raised to a shattering 600 mph

Overleaf: *Father and son: Sir Malcolm and Donald Campbell with* Bluebird, *1923*

and he realised that the only way forward was to re-engine the eleven-year-old Bluebird boat and continue on water. On 4 January 1967, after a disastrous winter, conditions seemed right for his eighth water speed record attempt, this time on the talismanic 300 mph barrier. Campbell and the Bluebird achieved a 297 mph first pass. Then, unaccountably, he failed to stop to refuel and let the wash die after his first run, and immediately headed back. The boat hit the wash and reared up into a 250 mph loop. Not until thirty-seven years later was Campbell's body recovered and, in a moving ceremony, buried in the Coniston churchyard.

The holy grail of the land speed record had always been Mach 1 or the sound barrier – around 760 mph but temperature-dependent. By 1983 the world land speed record had been raised to 633.468 mph for Britain by the Thrust2 team and in 1990 three teams announced challenges for the supersonic. The ThrustSSC team conceived the ultimate land speed record car – a 110,000 hp 54-foot twin-jet eleven-tonne monster – and recruited as driver RAF fighter pilot Andy Green, veteran of 1,000 fast jet hours. Unusually, the ThrustSSC was rear wheel steered, which required the development of completely new technology. The product of the IT age, it used extensive CFD (Computation Fluid Dynamics) and FEE (Finite Element Analysis) to develop the aerodynamics and the 9,000 rpm forged aluminium wheels.

Unfortunately for the team, market conditions had changed since the 1930s. In Malcolm Campbell's day a major innovative project like ThrustSSC would have been carried along on a wave of national enthusiasm, encouragement and finance. But in 1990s Britain the challenge of producing a supersonic land speed record car was greeted with fear and horror. With the largest corporate sponsor contributing just 8 per cent of the budget, the project was funded on a just-in-time basis over the internet and from direct merchandise sales to its 5,000-person supporters club.

By September 1997, however, the ThrustSSC car was ranged against the US Spirit of America. On 13 October Andy Green and ThrustSSC broke the sound barrier on land for the first time – but the crucial return run became impossible when the engine's exhaust flames burnt off the ThrustSSC brake parachutes and sent Green speeding brakeless past the Spirit of America camp faster than the Americans had ever been.

15 October 1997 was the magic day. By 10.30 a.m. Green had made two supersonic passes, each time turning the steering wheel hard right at 590 mph and holding it in full lock right up to 771 mph to maintain stability. He had driven through the sound barrier no fewer than five times, creating shockwaves which could be heard thirty miles away. After that Grand Prix racing would never seem the same again – and at 763.035 mph the land speed record looks set to belong to the British for a very long time to come.

Torvill and Dean's Boléro
Angela Rippon

Noon on 14 February 1984. An icy wind sliced through the skyscraper canyons surrounding Faneuil Hall Marketplace in Boston. Like the rest of America's East Coast population I was bundled up in duvet coat, ear muffs and fur boots against the wind-chill and pain of a Massachusetts winter. I'd been recording an interview with Peter Sellars, the Artistic Director of the Boston Shakespeare Company, for the Arts and Entertainment segment aired nightly on Channel Seven, the CBS affiliate station in Boston where I was the A and E correspondent. But now I was anxious to get back into the warmth of the studio. Not only because I had to check out final arrangements for the live outside broadcast I would be making later that evening from Symphony Hall, where the Boston Symphony Orchestra would be indulging themselves in a night of Musical Madness. But because within the hour I *had* to be near a television screen. Half a world away, in Sarajevo, Yugoslavia, the Winter Olympics were reaching a climax. Never mind all the Golds that had been clocked up by America, the Soviet Union, Austria, Switzerland, Italy and the rest of the Alpine nations. Like so many other Brits, regardless of where we were in the world that day or what time of the day or night it might be, I wanted to be *there*, to be actually watching *live* when Jayne Torvill and Christopher Dean walked out onto the ice to give what would undoubtedly be a world-beating performance.

Back in the office my assistant Marc Freeden had everything for the outside broadcast under control, so I popped my head around the door of the sports department to see how things were shaping up in Sarajevo. All the talk in the office was about the new football player who had been signed for the New England Patriots and how the city's ice hockey team, the Bruins, were doing in the league. Not a lot of interest was being shown in the pair of Eastern Europeans who were twirling around on the silent screen.

'Do me a favour, guys, and give me a shout when Torvill and Dean come on,' I asked. They promised they would, though I suspected that ice dancing wasn't all that high on their list of sporting priorities. Then I got back to working on my script for that evening's programme.

The shout 'Hey Ange, your guys are up!' got me out of my chair, across the office and in front of the screen before you could say 'double axle'. The sound was turned up, the Bruins and Patriots temporarily forgotten, and my American colleagues, I suspect out of curiosity more than anything else, crowded round to see what all the fuss was about.

There on the ice were two kneeling figures, colour-co-ordinated in purple, arms outstretched, gazing into each other's eyes. The familiar sound of the snare drum at the start of Ravel's *Boléro* cut through the silence.

And then it started. No fancy footwork, no blade-swirling fireworks to set the agenda and say 'OK: sit up and take notice because the champs have arrived'. Just a controlled,

sensuous merging of bodies, with Jayne slithering around Christopher's torso like a cobra.

This was ice dancing like we'd never seen before. For heaven's sake, it was a full thirty seconds before Christopher got off his knees and even put a blade to ice! But even in that opening Torvill and Dean had once again rewritten the rules on free-form skating, and we all recognised that we were about to see something quite extraordinary.

As the music pursued its relentless, pulsating beat in ever-mounting crescendo, they gave the performance of their lives. Their bodies moved in perfect harmony and unison, each mirroring the other to perfection. From a technical perspective, their fans had come to expect nothing less than the classy perfection that had made them World Champions the year before in Helsinki with their cheeky interpretation of the music from *Barnum*. But here was something new. The two faces we'd come to recognise beaming 2,000-watt smiles at the sheer joy of their art were now serious and tortured, reflecting the intensity of the ice ballet they were acting out. In place of showy flamboyance we watched a master class in the grace and ease of perpetual motion and total control. While their technique was flawless, their bodies oozed passion and raw emotion. It was a sizzling, erotic performance. Here were two tormented lovers baring their souls to the world, and they set the ice on fire.

When the music climaxed and they threw themselves onto the ice, for a split second you could have heard a heartbeat in that tiny office in Boston. Then, in unison with the audience in Sarajevo, we all burst into applause and I found my eyes were decidedly misty. I was being patted on the back as if *I'd* just performed what was later described as 'the finest four minutes of the Winter Olympics', and I must admit I felt that warm, patriotic glow most of us experience when the 'home team' slaughters the opposition.

But it wasn't over. Up came the first set of scores for technical excellence. A perfect six from three of the judges and 5.9s from the rest. Then artistic impression. The roar from the crowd and the expression on Jayne's face beat the television computer to the score line. Nine perfect sixes. Did any of us doubt it could ever have been anything less?

I don't recall much about the Boston Symphony concert that night, except that I know they didn't play Ravel's *Boléro* and that several of the audience congratulated me on 'your wonderful British skaters'. When I finally arrived home just before midnight and opened the door to my apartment, there was my husband with a large bunch of red roses. I hadn't seen him for two months, and the *Daily Mirror* had flown him over as an 'exclusive' surprise for me on Valentine's Day.

It was the perfect ending for a very special day, and yet another reason why I won't ever forget 14 February 1984.

Jayne Torvill and Christopher Dean dancing Boléro *at the 1984 Winter Olympics*

The cricket umpire
Dickie Bird

What is it that makes a good cricket umpire? And what makes the umpire such a great part of the game of cricket?

To be a good umpire requires many of the same qualities it takes to be a good player. You need to use common sense, consistency, application, dedication and concentration, and you need to show mental strength. Mental strength is perhaps the most important quality of all. If you believe in your ability it helps you to make correct decisions.

And once you've made your decision, you need to make it absolutely clear to the players. I've always made a point of announcing my decisions at the top of my voice – so much so that a batsman in one local match was clean bowled after hearing a no-ball called, not, as it turned out, by the umpire of his game, who immediately gave him out, but from up the road where I was umpiring a match at the county ground!

You need to stick to your decisions too. If the umpire makes a mistake he must forget it. That is history. As the late great umpire Syd Buller once said to me, the most important thing is the next ball being bowled. You must never waste time worrying about the past and you must never try to even things up. That just means you've made two mistakes instead of one.

Of course, it is also crucial that you make sure the game is played within the laws of the game. The play can be hard, but it has to be fair, and you are there to make sure the players show good sportsmanship. It is so very important that the umpire treats the players as professional men and tries to gain their respect.

That said, times have changed now as far as the umpire in the middle is concerned. I think the third umpire, on the camera in the stand, is the most important man at a cricket match now. Look at how many decisions he has to make: the close run-out; the stumpings; the hit wicket; the low catch to the ground; and if there is any problem with the boundary, the four and the six. That's six decisions in all. The men in the middle have only to make the LBW, the bat pad and the caught behind decisions.

Electronic aids have taken over, and the umpire in the middle, as we knew him, is finished. There have been too many occasions when the electronic eye has served to undermine rather than enhance the authority of the man in the middle. It's not a foolproof aid by any means, and more than one umpire has been proved right after the match in an out judgement he's had to overturn at the time because the electronic picture wasn't clear enough to support it. It is very sad. The umpire has been part of the game from its very beginnings. I would leave it to the umpires in the middle to make every decision in all aspects of the game. Their decision should always be final.

Making his decision clear: Dickie Bird umpires the England v. West Indies match at the Oval, May 1995

The umpire is a part of the whole game of cricket in a way that no electronic aid can ever be. Unlike most football referees, for example, most cricket umpires have played the game at first-class level themselves. They know it from the inside, and that kind of perspective shows itself in all sorts of ways. For instance, I always used to get to the ground early; I would be there at 8.00 a.m. for an 11.00 a.m. start. I used to have a long chat with the groundsman to see that everything was in order: the sight screens, the pitch, the markings, the boundary ropes and the many other things behind the scenes which go to ensure the smooth running of the game. (In fact, my early start almost got me into trouble in one of my first county games as an umpire, a Surrey versus Yorkshire match at the Oval. The game was due to start at 11.30, but I was terrified that I might be late and got to the Oval by six o'clock, only to find it locked. As I lobbed my bag over the gate and started to climb I was accosted by a local policeman, who took some persuading that I was who I said I was. Not even umpires, he said, turn up five and a half hours before a game.) There's so much more to umpiring than just making decisions on the field of play, crucial as that is.

Above all, though, umpiring is to be enjoyed. It's so important that you enjoy it. One of the golden rules is: always have a smile on your face. I've never had any difficulty with that part of the job description. I have some wonderful memories of my time as a county cricket and Test umpire, both on the field – umpiring World Cup finals, the Centenary Test Match, the Bicentenary Test match – and off it – travelling all over the world, meeting prime ministers, having lunch with the Queen. Even the more embarrassing memories – such as the time I stopped an England v. Australia Test match at Old Trafford because nature called, and I rushed off to the toilet to a great roar from the crowd – can make me smile in retrospect. Not to mention the county match when I forgot I was an umpire and not a player, and ran from behind the stumps to try to catch a high ball on the boundary. And what better illustration could there be than that of how deeply involved the umpire is with the match he umpires, how inseparably linked with the great game of cricket in which, from the very earliest days, he has played so central and indispensable a part?

The Vanwall
Robert Edwards

If one car can be said to encapsulate the greatness of British motor racing it is the Vanwall. In 1951, however, the vision on offer for the future of the racing car looked very different. At the Festival of Britain that year, pride of place went to the BRM, that flawed brainchild of pre-war racer Raymond Mays.

But one of the men who had helped fund that operation was Guy Anthony (Tony) Vandervell, the proprietor of Vandervell Products, an engine-bearing manufacturer based at Acton in London. Vandervell was no fool. However, he was opinionated, irascible to the point of rudeness and totally committed to his view of how the post-war British racing car should be built – and it was not, he had decided, a BRM. Not only had he conceived a profound distaste for some of the personalities involved in the hugely expensive BRM project. He also realised that if an enterprise such as this was to prosper, then someone – him – would have to manage it. Having first tried, and failed, to hijack the whole venture, he commenced on his own strategy.

Vandervell Products was basically an engine company – a point lost on some commentators, who entertained few hopes for the success of a home-grown product given the lead already enjoyed by Ferrari, Maserati and Daimler-Benz. They cited the examples of Connaught and BRM, both of which marques had shown promise, but neither of which had prospered. Vandervell saw things differently. In his opinion, Connaught was underfunded and BRM simply incompetent.

Given the vast amount of negative publicity which had accompanied the development of the BRM, Tony Vandervell resolved to keep strictly to his own agenda. Another of his interests lay in motorcycles: until 1954, in those happy days before anyone conceived that Japan could make any contribution to two-wheeled transport, he had been a director of the Norton Company. The Norton 500cc twin-cam engine was something of a benchmark in bike circles, mainly because the thrust toward mechanical efficiency had not been diverted by the use of supercharging. Vandervell's view, that four Norton cylinders mounted on a common crankcase might be a sensible jumping-off point for a new species of British racing car, was met with polite cynicism by the flat-earthers at Norton's HQ.

Famously, the cynics were wrong: by 1955, Vandervell had a car. It was technically underdeveloped, using as it did a proprietary chassis (by Cooper) and bodywork which was at best derivative, but with the full resources of Vandervell's R&D budget behind it, it was nothing if not a statement of intent.

At the end of 1955, however, Vandervell was to encounter Francis Albert Costin. Costin was moonlighting at the time. By day he was the chief development engineer at De Havillands; but after hours he had built a reputation as the designer of Colin Chapman's innovative Lotus sports racing cars, which were sweeping all before them in the smaller capacity events. Costin and Vandervell met at Oulton Park, where Costin was asked what he thought of Vandervell's pride and joy. His view, trenchantly expressed, was that 'the engine was fine, but the rest was rubbish'. Straightaway, Vandervell challenged him to improve upon it. Costin said he could, but that in order to exploit the advantages of aerodynamics which he felt would rescue the project, the car would need a new chassis which only Colin Chapman could design. Vandervell assented and the pair began work, Costin and Chapman being spurred to even greater efforts over the winter when Stirling Moss apparently endorsed Costin's opinion by opting to drive for Maserati for 1956 after his experience of driving the Cooper-chassised car in November 1955.

By the start of the 1956 season, they had finished. The resulting car was visually extraordinary, containing as it did every trademark of the Costin approach – an elegant teardrop shape wrapped around a sturdy space-frame structure penned by Chapman. The suspension was soft, the ground clearance huge, the gear change brutal, but the raw, if unsophisticated, power of the feral fuel-injected four-cylinder Vanwall engine was remarkable.

For 1957, Stirling Moss finally signed for Vanwall. His teammate was Tony Brooks, and in the summer they were joined by Stuart Lewis-Evans. As it turned out, the trio had a frustrating season, but they were all sufficiently impressed, not least by the commitment of Vandervell himself, to elect to persist with Vanwall into 1958.

That 1958 season was to mark the unargued ascendancy of Britain in the field of Formula 1, a position which it has never lost. It also saw a novelty in the form of a constructor's world championship. Vandervell had everything he needed to produce a double victory. He had green cars and British drivers. But against him was the might of Ferrari and a BRM which seemed to be coming up fast; and in the background was Cooper. (Maserati, alas, had succumbed to receivership and were no longer fielding works entries.) The victory of Stirling Moss's little Cooper in Argentina (a race which Vandervell, for technical reasons, did not attend) set the tone for the season, as Enzo Ferrari's iron grip upon the sport was, finger by finger, prised loose. But it would be the Vanwall that clinched it.

The matter came down to the wire at Casablanca in October 1958. Whether or not Stirling Moss would take the driver's title depended entirely upon the outcome of this single race. Moss had to win and set fastest lap (for which there was a single vital point), and the Ferrari of Mike Hawthorn had to come no better than third.

In the event, Stirling Moss did everything he could: he won the race and set fastest lap. But Hawthorn, still dispirited by the loss of his close friend Peter Collins in August, was allowed through by his teammate Phil Hill to take second place and the title. As expected, though, it was the Vanwall which carried the inaugural constructor's crown.

But the victory came at a heavy price. Poor Stuart Lewis-Evans had crashed and a week later succumbed to his dreadful burns, dying at East Grinstead hospital. Vandervell

had secured his prize and set the British Grand Prix industry on its way, but the emotional cost of it seems to have been way beyond him. Having given British motor racing its defining marque, and the international sport one of its greatest cars, he retired his team and returned to business. His achievements eclipsed by those of lesser men, he died in 1966.

Costin and Chapman's revolutionary Vanwall car being inspected on an early outing

Matthew Webb's cross-Channel swim
Duncan Goodhew

My daughter Victoria, six years old, is swimming her first length. She sets off down the 25-metre pool, sinking to that depth all young children manage where their nose is the only part of their frail little body above the surface of the water. It is a mystery to all parents how life can be sustained in this position underwater – and suddenly I am no longer a swimmer, but just another parent, stripping off, unable to contain myself as Victoria sinks deeper. But she carries on, seemingly oblivious of the vast, dwarfing expanse of water between her and the safety of dry land. How she makes that 25 metres, that first length, I will never know. But she does it, apparently defying all laws of physics and biology in the process. With her eyes glistening and a smile from ear to ear, she turns to me and cries triumphantly: 'France at last!'

The reference, of course, is to the English Channel, and the first person ever to swim across it, Captain Matthew Webb of Dawley in Shropshire, who achieved the feat in 1875 at the age of twenty-seven. But how can an event that seems almost trivial now have been so significant in its time, so universally esteemed, that it can still have such resonance for us today? The barrier Webb broke was more than the miles he swam, many as they were. There was instead something heroic, something beyond ordinary conception, about the very thought of the act.

In my book *Sink or Swim* I looked at the definition of success and came to the conclusion that success is as personal as your own fingerprint. It is only by setting out with a desire to get from A to B and succeeding that you acquire a sense of self-achievement. It is an event that has stretched you, creating anticipation, adrenalin and a defining moment. Has all the work, sacrifice and risk been worth it? Have I accomplished what I set out to achieve? In failure, will I be able to face those that I care for, my family, my friends, my peers and, of course, my adversaries? In success, I will walk tall and feel the power of what may be possible tomorrow.

'France at last!' Occasionally, that cry of accomplishment is heard around the world. No doubt every generation has someone who successfully captures the imagination of all who hear of their achievement. Perhaps this is a public quest, something we need in order to satisfy ourselves that there are still heroes and heroines, a yearning for something larger in life than one's own daily existence. Perhaps, too, it is a feeling that we should push the envelope, physically or intellectually, to prove that we are superior to our ancestors, that life is linear and that the line is up. I once heard potential described as being like a thought that has not yet come into the mind – that is as true of us individually as it is collectively of the human race. Somehow a great individual accomplishment gives us a

'Nothing great is easy': Captain Matthew Webb in the year he became the first man to swim the Channel

collective feeling that we as human beings have achieved something extraordinary. We feel in some way a part of it, even if only as a witness, a spectator in a packed sports stadium who blinks at the crucial moment; it still happened while *we were there*.

Such moments are not always the product of mass movements or national budgets. Occasionally, and incredibly, a lone individual with few resources audaciously catches that same wave of human emotion and rides high, inspiring and warming us. Captain Matthew Webb's moment was born out of unimaginable change. The industrial revolution had changed our view of the world through steam, the eighteenth and nineteenth centuries' equivalent of atomic power. Steam, and the machines it drove, changed lives. Distances were drawn in by steam-powered ships and locomotives. Australia seemed suddenly closer. London to Edinburgh was a day trip. You can almost hear the Victorians, riding this wave of achievement, ask 'What shall we do next? What else can we achieve? Where are our limits?'

Captain Webb rode that wave literally. At 12.56 p.m. on 24 August 1875, rubbed down with porpoise oil and clad in daring scarlet silk swimming trunks, he set off to swim from England to France. The English Channel had kept countless enemies from invading Britain. It defined England, symbolising her difference from her European neighbours. The thought that a person could now swim the same distance that had kept Napoleon at bay – twenty-two miles of cold, choppy water, sucked down through the Channel from the North Sea to meet the Atlantic Ocean – must have seemed impossible to many. Indeed, it would be thirty-six years before Webb's mighty feat was repeated, since when fewer than 500 people have managed this demanding, draining swim. Captain Webb was not only the first but remains still one of only a handful to have swum the Channel breaststroke. Open water swimmers now plough through the sea using the freestyle stroke, which was then still to be invented. Freestyle, or Australian crawl as it was originally called, not only allows a swimmer to drive through the waves with greater ease; it is also a far more efficient and faster stroke, and thus reduces the time and energy spent in the Channel's frigid waters.

As he set out from Dover that August day, having failed to complete the swim a few weeks before, Webb must have had many doubts. Had he judged the tides correctly so that they would help him rather than sucking him back? With each stroke he would have raised his head, breathing carefully to avoid taking in water from the waves. With each stroke he would have caught a glimpse of the open expanse of cold, grey, murky water stretching remorselessly in front of him. As the sun set, the cold must have bitten deep. The horizon would have started to blend with the then inky-black water where wave dissolved into sky. Then hours of chilling, lonely darkness.

Webb took coffee on a regular basis until he was stung by a jellyfish. He then accepted brandy, the medicine of the day, to help him on his way. Gradually, cold and fatigue took its toll on his stroke rate, which dropped from twenty a minute to sixteen, occasionally falling as low as twelve. What a relief it must have been to catch, from the crest of a wave, his first glimpse of France – so close, yet so far. The tide had pushed him up and down the Channel, making him swim an estimated thirty-nine miles. As he slowed, the last few miles must have seemed an eternity to him. I know one swimmer who, unable to punch the tide, was stranded for six hours until it allowed him to strike shore. Others within sight of France succumb to exhaustion or the ravages of the sea-sickness that often grips a swimmer unaccustomed to the roll generated by the Channel swell. Not Captain Webb. Thirty-nine and three-quarter hours after plunging in at Dover he alighted from the water as one of those singularly rare 'firsts' whose achievements strike deep into the hearts and minds of men.

In a sense we are still who we were then. It is still true that travelling from A to B, if it's the right A to B, and given the right conditions, can capture our imaginations, inspire us, and fill us with awe in a sense of our own humanity. It is not actually the feat but rather the sense of the feat that makes the difference. Fundamental to awe is fear – fear of the water, fear of invasion across the Channel, or simply fear of failure and death. Perhaps the real national heroes will always be those who risk everything to master their fears, in the process gaining the adulation of the public.

Sadly, as Captain Webb found out, living on such a peak can have devastating consequences: it is the event, not the seeking of adulation, which is the legitimate goal of man. Webb drew crowds in America for his demonstrations of endurance swimming in pools, sometimes swimming 4,000 lengths at a stretch. As time went on, though, his swims became more and more desperate. Finally, in 1883, without financial backing or for that matter much publicity, he attempted to swim across Niagara Falls. It was a suicidal venture. In front of only a couple of hundred spectators Captain Webb disappeared into a whirlpool at the head of the Falls, leaving behind his wife and two small children.

But let us remember him for his extraordinary and truly exceptional first achievement. As his epitaph reads on the memorial to him in Dawley, his birthplace, 'Nothing great is easy'.

The twin towers of Wembley
Hunter Davies

In the programme for the very first FA Cup final at Wembley, between Bolton Wanderers and West Ham United on 28 April 1923, there is a section modestly entitled 'The Greatest Arena in the World'. It boasted how 'this vast stadium, the largest in the world, the most comfortable, the best equipped, holds more than 125,000 people. In area it equals the Biblical city, Jericho.'

How did they know that? Was Jericho ever officially measured? Bit of a liberty, surely. But they needed to bang the drum about this new and wonderful stadium for many reasons, least of all a footballing one. At the previous year's Cup final, held at Stamford Bridge, the crowd had been only 53,000 to see Huddersfield beat Preston 1–0. They were therefore somewhat worried about whether 125,000 football fans would turn up to the new venue.

But the main reasons for all the boasting were architectural and imperial. The building was truly awesome, the biggest ferro-concrete construction ever built. More than 250,000 tons of earth had been dug out of a greenfield site, 25,000 tons of concrete were poured in, 2,000 tons of structural steel reinforced it and half a million rivets held it all together. The result was 890 feet long, 650 feet wide and 126 feet high to the top of its twin towers. The towers were symbolic – and hollow – harking back to an iron tower which had been erected on the site a few years earlier and was meant to rival the Eiffel Tower in Paris till its foundations moved and it had to be pulled down.

The stadium was completed in just 300 days, which is miraculous in itself. A whole battalion of soldiers was brought in to march up and down on the terraces to make sure the structure would stand up to all the vibrations and feet of roaring fans.

Yet the stadium itself was only one part of an even greater and more glorious creation, the British Empire Exhibition, covering 216 acres and containing fifteen miles of roads. There were about thirty other massive buildings to house exhibitions, as well as parks, theatres, lakes, funfairs. After a hideous crippling war, Britain was determined to show the rest of the world that it was back in business – and of course top of the tree once more. 'Come to Wembley', so the programme continued. 'Visit the British Empire Exhibition in 1924. You will discover more about your country and your Empire than could ordinarily be learned in a lifetime, for this British Empire Exhibition is indeed the most wonderful, the most romantic enterprise in history.'

In the event, 200,000 people turned up for the first game at Wembley, including King George V – and most of them appear to have got in, besieging the turnstiles, pushing through barriers. It's a wonder that Wembley did not begin with a national disaster. But thanks to the good nature of the crowd, and a policeman on a white horse who kept cool, no one got killed. The policeman became a legend in his lifetime – well, famous for at least fifteen minutes in all the papers next day. Bolton won 2–0. Everyone was well pleased, apart from West Ham fans.

After the Empire Exhibition, which lasted for two years, 1924 and 1925, all the imperial bits and pieces, exhibitions and displays, were destroyed or disposed of. The Palestine Pavilion became a laundry in Glasgow. The East Africa building was turned into a jam factory. Several cafés were taken away and re-erected as Bournemouth and Boscombe FC's grandstand. Only the stadium itself remained, proud and erect, the venue for every Cup final and almost every major sporting event held in Britain from then on. In 1940 it was used to house evacuees from Dunkirk who had nowhere else to sleep. In 1948 national boasting got back into its stride when the Olympics were held there, one of the main routes to the stadium becoming known as Olympic Way.

After the war, Wembley's twin towers became recognised by every football fan wherever football was played. In Britain there were social and geographical symbols associated with Wembley too. For many working-class northerners and Scotsmen, this was the only time they ever came to London – on day trips, their annual ritual, to see their team or country play. The London press portrayed these northern hordes as rough aliens, from another planet, which in the 1930s, during the years of unemployment, they often seemed.

I loved going to Wembley. I always went on the Tube – which I normally avoid – going from Finchley Road to Wembley Park. Whatever the occasion, the fans were well-behaved, cheerful, unaggressive, even when well-oiled, which you can't say about normal games. They were just so pleased to be there. Reaching Wembley, physically as well as metaphorically, was an end and a pleasure in itself.

Catching that first glimpse of the twin towers, my heart used to give an extra little beat. Climbing up and around the concrete steps, though, that wasn't such fun. Inside the bowels of the building, over the years it became dirty, scruffy, smelly, with queues for all refreshments, which were horrible anyway. But ah, when you made your way to your seat, that first flash of bright green was blinding, wonderful, inspiring, after the grey of the concrete approach and of life itself.

I always felt I was communing with the football world when I took my seat at Wembley. I was not only part of the Wembley crowd, but part of history, of the nation, and of the whole football tribe, regardless of who I was watching or even the result – whether it was England, Scotland, Spurs or Carlisle United. I did in fact see CUFC play twice at Wembley, in something called the Auto Windscreens Shield. Carlisle is my home town. While sitting there at the Carlisle end, I found myself among people I was at school with yet hadn't seen for forty years. Wembley did have its uses.

As I write, Wembley is closed, the towers at least about to be pulled down. As a stadium, the old one had outlived its usefulness. Inside it had become nasty, cold, brutal, uncomfortable. But whatever its fate, whatever replaces it, inside the minds and memories of all football fans it will live on, an inspiration for ever. *Wem-bur-lee*! *Wem-bur-lee*!

Overleaf: 'The greatest arena in the world': the twin towers of Wembley Stadium

TURNSTILES
◄ A.B.C.D.E.F.
G.H.J.K.L.M. ►

Jimmy 'The Whirlwind' White
Andrew Graham-Dixon

Jimmy White, who proved that there is more to being great at a game than winning its greatest prizes, was not just the most entertaining, cheeky, inventive and outrageously talented snooker player of his generation. He was (and remains) one of the true heroes of a quintessentially British game: the personification of snooker's slightly seedy glamour, its dishevelled gentlemanliness and unlikely grace.

The cliché has it that White is the greatest player never to win the World Championship, the implication being that there is something of the choker about him. There may be a tiny element of truth there (although perhaps a fairer explanation is pure bad luck), but the danger is that it makes White sound like one of those dreary golfers who keep finishing second but never quite win a Major. He has been far more to his sport than a gifted, gallant loser. White, as much as anyone – including even his mentor, the volatile Irish showman, two-times World Champion Alex Higgins – helped to take the game out of the shadows of the snooker hall and turn it into a compelling form of mass spectacle. He changed people's attitudes to the sport that he played. He also changed his fellow-competitors' attitudes to it, fostered a new and aggressively high-scoring style of play, and so played a vital role in giving snooker its modern shape and character.

Ever since he started playing, as a truant from school in his early teens, hiding from the police and from school inspectors underneath Table 9 at Zan's Snooker Hall in Tooting, South London, it was obvious to all who knew him that White was that rare thing in sport: a natural. In his early years, before he could afford his own cue, he would improvise. Legend has it that he hustled thousands from unsuspecting punters while playing with a broken leg, using a walking stick as his cue. Steve Davis, a snooker player of a rather different type, recalled seeing White make several century breaks with that unlikely implement. Davis is not renowned for his flights of fancy, so the story seems likely to be true. Perhaps the unorthodox way in which he learnt to play helps to explain why, once he got a proper cue in his hand, White made the game look so ridiculously easy.

White never dominated snooker in the way that first Steve Davis and then Stephen Hendry – the two World Champions who did most to prevent him becoming one – managed to do. He never dominated it in terms of trophies won and winnings earned (although he won and by all accounts gambled away a small fortune over the years). But he dominated it nonetheless, through the sheer force of his personality, through his imagination and skill and audacity.

If one shot sums him up (which of course one shot cannot do) it is perhaps the final pink of the clearance he made in the last frame of his 1984 semi-final in the Benson &

Hedges Masters, against the brilliant Canadian player Kirk Stevens. Stevens, his career yet to be ruined by cocaine-addiction, had contributed more than his share to the match, which was one of snooker's classic confrontations. Dressed in an all-white suit of dubious taste but considerable flamboyance, he was John Travolta in *Saturday Night Fever* to White's Artful Dodger, lean and sallow, with a hungry, ferret-like look to him. The pair had traded centuries, and with the score standing at 4–3 in White's favour, Stevens had made what still stands as one of the most remarkable maximum 147 breaks ever seen in competition, potting an all-around-the-table green to stay alive and managing somehow to get position on the last black from a fiendishly difficult position on the pink. Stevens boogied with the referee, the crowd went crazy: 4–4. But still White came back to win the match and, with more than enough points under his belt to ensure victory in the final frame, decided to have some fun with the penultimate ball: that pink.

It was close to the baulk cushion, about nine inches away from the pocket. The white was about a foot away, itself just off the baulk cushion. White slammed the pink in and followed through with the cue almost far enough to dislocate his shoulder, in the process imparting a phenomenal amount of backspin to the white. Because he struck it low on the left-hand side, he also put running side on the cue ball. As the pink rocketed home, the white fizzed off the left-hand side cushion and came back down the table in a geometry-defying virtual straight line. Having somehow persuaded the ball to take this unlikely trajectory, running towards the top cushion to the left of the black, White stood patiently watching it, like the master of some exceptionally well trained dog. He prepared to play his next shot, on the black, while the cue ball was still moving. It still looked, at the time, as if the white was travelling much too fast to leave any kind of position on the black. But as it hit the top cushion, the running side turned to check side, stopping the white almost dead and turning it back neatly to finish, docilely, perfect weight on the black. For weeks afterwards, amateurs in snooker halls up and down the country were recreating the position and trying – in vain – to duplicate the shot.

That pink was a 'flair shot', played to entertain the crowd once the match was already won. But White often gave the impression, even when a frame was still alive, that he was as interested in the beauty of the game as he was in winning it. He would seemingly prefer one shot to another on the grounds of its elegance and play it for the satisfaction of seeing its charming geometry enacted. That is why so many of the matches in which he was involved were so open and entertaining. White could play good safety, but his instinct was always for attack: leaving the colours on their spots, opening the reds, taking the chance of a cannon here or a nudge there to improve the position. So when his opponents got chances they were often good chances. He certainly had the ability to freeze an opponent out of the game, as Steve Davis so often did. But he lacked the inclination, and the necessary meanness of spirit. He loved the game too much to ruin it for the sake of victory. His curious ability to bring out the best in those who played him was most in evidence during the several World Championship finals (six in all) which he contested and lost. In only one of those finals (1993, when he lost 16–5 to Stephen Hendry) did White

actually play badly, and in two others (1984, when Davis beat him 18–16; and 1991, when John Parrott beat him 18–11) his opponent chose the two days of the final to play the very best match snooker of his life.

White stands out for having played at the highest level – unlike anyone else in the game – during no fewer than three distinct eras of snooker. In 1982, when he was only twenty, the considerably older Alex Higgins made a miracle comeback against him from 15–14 and 50 points down in the semi-final of the World Championship. Higgins won 16–15 and went on to take the title easily – as White surely would have done, had he won that match – against the then elder statesman of the game, Ray Reardon. White may have been good enough to win the World title for two years previous to that, but had chosen to contest the World Amateur title instead. After that he witnessed the long years of Davis' ascendancy, almost toppling him in a tremendous final in 1984. As Davis faded, White seemed only to get stronger. But it was then his misfortune to get to the final five years in a row, only to come up on four occasions against the formidable Stephen Hendry.

Hendry remains, both statistically and in terms of match-playing temperament, the finest player in the history of snooker. Perhaps White was unlucky to have to live in his shadow during so much of the early 1990s (he lost the final to the Scot in 1990, 1992, 1993 and 1994). But White's relationship to the brilliant young player who defeated him so often was not simply that of vanquished foe to victor. Because if it had not been for the example of White's attacking play, the flair and aggressiveness that he had brought to the game, the shots he had shown his disbelieving contemporaries that it was possible to play, then Hendry would never have developed the brilliantly punishing style that he did. Snooker is a game which changes and evolves cumulatively, as new shots enter the repertoire and new approaches to break-building come into favour. But it was White's distinction to have altered the consensus of professional players' whole *approach* to snooker. Thanks to the brilliance of his example, out-and-out attack became the preferred style of a new generation of player.

So although he lost to Hendry, White was simultaneously witnessing the triumph of his own moral and imaginative influence on the game. And even if, as seems increasingly likely, he never does win the World Championship, his spirit triumphs year in and year out. The force of his legacy has been felt more strongly than ever in recent years. The players yet younger than Hendry who have since dominated snooker – John Higgins, Mark Williams, and the incomparable Ronnie O'Sullivan – have done so by cleaving yet more firmly to White's example. Only the greatest sportsmen change the very sport they play. While there was snooker before Jimmy White, and there was snooker after Jimmy White, they were not the same game.

Jimmy White during the 1994 Embassy World Snooker Championships at The Crucible, Sheffield

Wimbledon Centre Court
Virginia Wade

Centre Court, Wimbledon – the very name has the ring of magic. Location, prestige, fame and emotion meet here to create what must surely be the most valuable rectangle of grass in the world. It might in reality be just an inanimate object, a patch of elementary horticulture housed in a concrete frame, but I would swear that it has a heart and a soul.

The magnetism of the Centre Court is palpable. On visits to Wimbledon, even in the depths of winter when there is not a person in sight, I have to take a peek at it. Without its white lines and with the dark green of the longer grass, it appears as lush as velvet. There is no feeling of emptiness in there, as there usually is in a deserted stadium; there is only intimacy. It's as though one is privileged to see the real self of the court, not just the public persona with its make-up applied, its manicure perfect and the full royal regalia lovingly in place, ready for the festivities to begin.

Eighty years ago, at the inauguration of the current Church Road site of the All England Lawn Tennis and Croquet Club, the Centre Court was unveiled as the perfect stadium. It inherited the name from its predecessor at the Worple Road site, which truly was a central court with the others surrounding it. Here at Wimbledon there would not be a shadow from the sun till 7.00 p.m. at championship time, there would be a perfect view from every seat (except those few that had stanchions semi-obscuring theirs) and the 'garden-style' back to the benches made for plenty of comfort. Rain would be kept at bay by the roof that covered most of the 10,000 seats, even if the other 4,000-odd spectators in standing room would have to make do with umbrellas. The roof was certainly needed: that first Wimbledon at the new grounds began with a rain delay and became the wettest championship on record at the time. So deluged was it that the men's final was only completed on the third Monday and the doubles finals on the third Wednesday!

Tennis was experiencing a meteoric rise. During the First World War the young men were away at the Front and the young women were involved in war work at home. Deprivation fuelled the need for recreation and sport. In 1919 Worple Road was besieged by new international stars, with the arrival of a handful of athletic young Australian men and, above all, the debut of the twenty-year-old Frenchwoman Suzanne Lenglen. Her youthful exuberance, dazzling performances and extraordinary skill brought record crowds flocking to see her win her first singles title in dramatic style against the supreme champion Dorothea Lambert Chambers. King George and Queen Mary were there, and before long the whole world wanted to be there too – which is precisely why the new facility at Church Road was built in 1922.

Virginia Wade after winning the Ladies Singles Championship at Wimbledon in July 1977

Despite the appalling weather at those inaugural championships, not to mention a three-hour delay before the ladies' final, Suzanne made her usual extravagant entrance to the Centre Court, in silk frock with a fur coat bundled around her, and proceeded to demolish her opponent, Molla Mallory, in twenty-six minutes with the loss of only two games. Story has it that the pressure of always winning was already taking its toll of her nervous disposition and that while she waited for the sky to clear she was in rare form, pacing round and round the dressing-room, re-applying lipstick and make-up. After all, this was a match of supreme importance: the first chance for Suzanne to avenge the defeat Mrs Mallory had had the temerity to impose upon her (albeit by a default) the previous year at Forest Hills. This was the fourth of the six titles Suzanne was to accrue at Wimbledon. Her last appearance was on the golden anniversary of the championships, in 1926. Then, owing to a mix-up in communications, she kept Queen Mary waiting for half an hour in an infamous incident that precipitated her retirement into the professional ranks.

Despite the departure of the 'Divine Goddess', the jubilee championships shone with new stars, including a British lady champion, Kitty McKane Godfree, who won her second title, beating the glamorous Lili de Alvarez in the final. This royal Wimbledon was graced by many members of the Royal Family, one – the future King George VI – even taking part as a doubles player.

The Golden Wimbledon came to an end, but not the golden age of tennis. The next kings of the game were the so-called four musketeers (Henri Cochet, René Lacoste, Jean Borotra and Toto Brugnon) who, together with Bill Tilden, ruled the men's court. The queen of the game was Helen Wills Moody, who racked up an awesome eight titles. Fred Perry, the great athletic Englishman, followed the French players to dominate the tennis world, winning three consecutive Wimbledon trophies before turning pro and opening the way for Don Budge to take the championship (and the Grand Slam).

During the Second World War Wimbledon ground to a halt for five years. It became a civil defence centre, while chickens were raised in the shade of the Centre Court. But the lawns stayed in good shape, the ivy continued to grow on the walls of the court, and when the gates opened again the show continued as normal. The Americans, who had been least affected by the hostilities, fielded a string of winners – Jack Kramer, Louise Brough and the brilliant diminutive Maureen Connolly. Then came a tidal wave of Australian champions, with Sedgman leading the way and Rosewall, Hoad, Laver and Emerson hard on his heels.

I first became aware of Wimbledon when I was still a tennis-mad teenager in South Africa, a country where TV did not exist but imagination ran high. When we returned to England to live, my heart leapt when I found our home was to be a rented house in Wimbledon, right up the road from the AELTC. The very next morning after we arrived, in the middle of January, I ran down to get a glimpse of the hallowed shrine. Alas, my investigation was stalled at the wrought iron gates, which were firmly locked, but later that year my ultimate dream of getting to the Centre Court, albeit as a school-uniformed spectator in standing room, came true. I followed all the players avidly, but my favourites were the graceful Maria Bueno and the superhuman Rod Laver. The next year, as the baby of the tournament, I played in the championships, winning a round, and the following year made my debut on the Centre Court in the second round against Ann Haydon. Was I ever nervous! When my father read the news to me from his newspaper that morning, I literally fell down the stairs. I lost, but I played well – and at least there was no school that day!

Centre Court became my home, though not always a comfortable one. Perhaps I worshipped it too much, and didn't believe I was worthy of all those superstars whose spirits dwelt there. Eventually when I had my final to play, I went in early and sat quietly attuning myself to its grandeur and rhythm, to the calm that would soon turn into a throbbing pulse. At my victory, I felt truly one with the essence of the court, with each and every member of the crowd. It wasn't just me who had won. The energy of everyone there surged through me. I was just a small instrument of the gods of the Centre Court.

The court has witnessed so many champions, such drama, so much sweat and effort, determination and talent. There will always be debate about which was the greatest match, the most worthy winner. Was the Borg–McEnroe final in 1980 superior to that of Rafter–Ivanisevic in 2001? Was Rod Laver a greater champion than Pete Sampras? Will Martina Navratilova's nine titles stand as the ladies' record, or can a Venus Williams break it? The Boris Beckers, the Steffi Grafs, the Margaret Courts, the great Grand Slam winners – all will continue to dazzle the Centre Court like the panoply of shooting stars from the recent Leonid meteors.

Each year the patchwork quilt of brilliance will grow a little. Some things will change – the attire of the spectators, their manner, the style of the players. But as with the constant renewal of cells in a human body, so the Centre Court will be reborn with every championship, its appeal at once more modern and yet timeless, a pantheon where the gods of tennis will continue to fight for their place in history.

Wisden Cricketers' Almanack
Stephen Moss

Does Wisden exist to be read? I only ask because it hadn't struck me until I sat down to write this essay (or, perhaps, love letter) that I had not yet properly read my 2001 Wisden. I have fondled it, felt its impressive heft (1,648 pages), tucked a copy of the averages from the 2001 English season into it, but I haven't actually read it. I bought it, of course, on the first day of that 2001 season – it always appears in early April as herald of a new cricketing year, the past eliding with the present in a way that exemplifies cricket's continuities, its desire for seamlessness (except on balls). I bought it and then put it next to the identical-looking volume from 2000 (a mere 1,600 pages, even though it had the onerous task of marking the passing of a cricketing century). And there it has sat since, barely consulted (now, let me think, how many runs did Baroda beat Bihar by in Super League Group B of the Ranji Trophy? ... and who is that promising leg-spinner at Charterhouse?). No doubt I looked at the beautifully produced colour photographs, read the section on my beloved Glamorgan ('somewhat disappointing this season, the county nevertheless promises much next year' or some variant thereon), paused to note a rather uninspiring batch of 'cricketers of the year', but then slid it onto the shelf beside its predecessors, gleamingly yellow and endlessly reassuring.

Wisden, you see, is not really for reading, it's for collecting; it is less a book than a brick, and when people talk about building a collection they really mean it. Wisdens do not merely furnish a room; a full set would enable you to build a sturdy shed. Visit a cricket-loving man of a certain age and there they will be – shelf-fuls of squat, fat volumes (brown before dust-wrappers were introduced in 1965, yellow thereafter), arranged in date order, the great game encapsulated. They provide a kind of emotional security in a disordered and dangerous world. Buy the 2001 volume and you possess the entire game for the previous year, the scores of every first-class match in every cricket-playing country, the date of birth and death of every notable cricketer, the laws of the game, all significant Test and first-class records. It gives you the world – a world that, despite the Hansie Cronje match-fixing affair, still makes sense. Buy the entire set – an uninterrupted run from 1864 – and you can possess the universe.

These days, however, emotional security does not come cheap. The inflationary point is usefully made by referring to an article on the history of Wisden published in the 1963 centenary edition of the almanack (note that all-important archaic 'k') by L E S Gutteridge (note, too, the initials – Wisden is a world of men with initials rather than first names). He points out that a complete set auctioned at Sotheby's in 1937 fetched £33, that in 1954 a set went for £145, and that at the time of writing his

The 'Little Wonder': John Wisden, c.1850, by William Bromley

centenary history a set in good condition would cost £250. I asked a bookseller friend what a set would sell for now, and he estimated £40,000 to £50,000, depending on its condition. He thought there were some thirty to fifty sets in private hands and that 400 to 500 people (mainly men with three initials) were actively collecting sets.

Even though I only have two initials, when resources admit I intend to join those determined collectors. I have dutifully bought every almanack since 1979 as they appeared and picked up a few others second-hand, but that barely constitutes a beginning. The post-war volumes are easy, even though they disappear from second-hand bookshops pretty smartly. This is the flat road. The hills begin before the Second World War and then the peaks loom: the war-rationed volumes of 1915 and 1916 (the latter almost did not appear and, it is claimed, only came out because W G Grace had died in 1915 and 'The Champion' had to be given a fitting send-off); the extremely rare volume of 1875 when fewer copies than usual were printed; and the precious first Wisden of 1864, the cricketing equivalent of a Shakespeare First Folio.

So difficult is it to get the first fifteen Wisdens that they have been reprinted in facsimile. Of the £40,000-plus outlay for a set, more than half would go on acquiring originals of those fifteen, even assuming they came up for sale. But the facsimiles would not really tempt me. I would want the original battered 1864 copy, with its secret history, and that 1875 rarity. I still, I hope, have half a lifetime left for the quest. Wisden is frequently referred to as the 'cricketer's bible', but it is more holy grail: acquiring the set promises to let you in on some secret, admits you to some cricketing elect. Or so it seems to us believers. Life, the universe and everything – though the answer is not 42 but 139, the number of the 2002 almanack.

Gutteridge's survey makes clear the competition Wisden had in the first thirty years from other annuals and almanacs. John Wisden himself (known as the 'Little Wonder' in his playing days) was a fast off-break bowler who once took ten wickets in an innings, all clean-bowled. He owned a sports equipment shop near Leicester Square and started the almanack in the year after he retired from the game, principally to advertise his sports goods. The first volume ran to 112 pages and, as Gutteridge remarks, 'contained a good deal of delightful, but quite extraneous, matter – such as the rules of knur and spell, a brief history of China, the rules for playing the game of bowls, the winners of the Derby, Oaks and St Leger, and sundry other "discrete" information on canals, British societies, the Wars of the Roses, and coinage'. All this for one shilling, the price at which the almanack was sold until 1915! No wonder it was such a success.

John Wisden died, aged fifty-seven, in 1884, but his company went on publishing it until 1937, when the ravages of the Depression forced it to sell out to Whitakers. In 1979, Whitakers sold it to the Macdonald publishing company, owned by Robert Maxwell, who threatened to remodel it along the lines of the Rothmans sports annuals. The men with initials fought a successful rearguard action and wrested it from Maxwell, re-establishing the imprint of John Wisden & Co. Since 1993 it has been published under the benign patronage of the cricket-loving millionaire philanthropist Paul Getty.

Wisden today is not merely an institution but – dread word – a brand. As well as the almanack, there is a magazine (*Wisden Cricket Monthly*), the inevitable website (www.wisden.com), an Australian version (in baggy-cap green rather than yellow) and several spin-off books, the most useful of which is the series of complete Test match scorecards in chronological order. But the almanack remains the core. There have been fourteen editors in its near-140-year history, with two of them – Sydney Pardon from 1891 to 1925 and Norman Preston from 1952 to 1980 – managing more than sixty years between them. That continuity has been central to Wisden's success: it has changed when it had to (new owners Whitakers restructured the book to make it more user-friendly in 1938 and editor Matthew Engel dusted away some of the reactionary cobwebs when he became editor in 1993), but each volume is recognisably part of the series. The reader of 1864 would not be too startled by the 2002 edition, even if he was inconvenienced by the bulk and distressed by the price (£35.00).

Gutteridge's account of Wisden's first hundred years ends with an anecdote about a Yorkshireman called K A Auty, who spent most of his life in the US, where he resided, with a large collection of cricketana. 'He kept his complete set of Wisden under his bed,' writes Gutteridge. 'He could then, having made himself properly comfortable, forget his maturing bills and overdue argosies, dip down and take at random any volume that came to hand. He was often found perusing the same volume hours later.' After finishing Gutteridge's article, I skipped 300 pages to look at how Glamorgan had fared in the 1962 season. I read through the scores of their home games, which are printed sequentially, and became interested in a match played against Middlesex at Newport (my home town and, sadly, no longer a venue for Glamorgan matches) in July: a dull draw, but who is this R A Gale who scored 200 for Middlesex? The Middlesex section is unforthcoming: an opening batsman, clearly, who enjoyed a reasonable season (he averaged 38.14) and was good enough to keep the twenty-year-old Mike Brearley out of the team. Oh, and he was born in Old Warden, Bedfordshire on 10 December 1933. But what happened to him, did he ever make another double-hundred, and how quickly did the England captain-to-be Brearley supersede him as opening bat? I don't have the volumes from the mid-1960s and now urgently need them to tie up these loose ends. My quick glance at the Glamorgan results has, in a moment, transported me to the struggles of forty years ago. Like Auty, a cricket-mad Yorkshireman in a foreign land, I am back in a world I love and can understand, where past and present exist on terms of easy intimacy and mutual regard. I may be there some time.

England's 1966 World Cup victory
Hunter Davies

I was there in 1966. And I still have my ticket to prove it – Seat 37, Row 9, Entrance 36, Turnstile K. It was a not to be forgotten day, which about half a million English persons have regularly not forgotten, their first-hand memories crystal clear, even though there were only 93,000 present in the flesh.

It's strange that I held on so tightly to my ticket, keeping it safely all these years. At the time it was common to collect football programmes, but not football tickets. In fact, it wasn't until recently that I came across anyone else who had kept their 1966 final ticket. I noticed it in a catalogue priced at £150. Not bad for a piece of paper which originally cost £5.

I got mine through a friend, the late James Bredin, who at the time was managing director of Border TV in Carlisle. He was not particularly a football fan, but had access to some tickets through his position. I have a memory of a hospitality suite, not at Wembley itself but in a block nearby. I had to report there first, had a few jars, then went with James in his chauffeur-driven car to the stadium. Never done it in such style, before or since.

I was also at England's semi-final, a 2–1 win against Portugal, which was probably the best match, for pure football, in the whole of the 1966 competition. Bobby Charlton was outstanding, scoring both of England's goals. After his second, he received the handshakes of Eusebio and other Portuguese players – even though the game had not finished. How often do you see that?

In the final, Charlton was not so evident. Alf Ramsey told him to go out and mark Franz Beckenbauer – not knowing that Helmut Schoen, the German manager, had detailed Beckenbauer to mark Charlton. Before kick-off, Ramsey caused a bit of a surprise by omitting Jimmy Greaves, whom most experts had expected to play. He'd been in the first three games, against Uruguay, Mexico and France, then Geoff Hurst, relatively untried at this level, had come in and the boy had done well. There had even been suggestions that Ramsey might not play Bobby Moore in the finals, as he'd been rather naughty on an overseas tour, breaking Ramsey's strict curfew. Some thought that Norman Hunter, well known for biting legs, might get Moore's place.

Despite clutching my little ticket, and clearly remembering most of the build-up to the day, the game itself went in a flash. It was so exciting, so dramatic, if not quite a classic.

Germany scored first, after thirteen minutes. Hurst equalised, six minutes later. Martin Peters put England ahead with just twelve minutes left. But in the ninetieth minute Germany got a scrambled goal to draw level: 2–2. The game then had to go to extra time, the first time it had happened in a World Cup final since 1934.

A team who has just equalised always has the psychological advantage, but out on the pitch, apparently – I couldn't hear a word – Ramsey pointed at the German players and barked 'Look at them! They're finished!' In the hundredth minute Hurst got his controversial goal, the one which for years Germans maintained had not crossed the line. Then Hurst got another, making it 4–2 and ensuring a clear win. In 1996 Beckenbauer admitted England had deserved it: 'Bobby Charlton had at that time lungs like a horse. I never remember being so exhausted as I was at the finish that afternoon.'

England were the better team and performed well after a slow and iffy start to the finals – their opening game, the one against Uruguay, had been a boring 0–0 draw. They were also helped by the fact that the Italians got stuffed by North Korea, one of the biggest upsets in World Cup football ever, and didn't even make it to the quarter-finals. Brazil's artistry also let them down, and they too failed to make the quarter-finals, being beaten by Hungary and Portugal. The other likely teams, from Russia, Uruguay and Argentina, suffered disciplinary problems. England, so it was thought, had also been greatly helped by being the host nation and playing all their games at Wembley.

But we all rejoiced, street parties took place, heads were held high, flags waved, and we all felt it confirmed – what we always really knew deep down – that England, who gave football to the world, were still the greatest. Various foreign johnnies had in recent years given us the occasional bit of a kicking, such as the Hungarians in 1953, beating England 6–3 at Wembley, and – oh ignominy – the United States, who in 1950 had defeated England 1–0 in England's first ever World Cup. But we had dismissed these as freak results, passing aberrations, unlikely ever to happen again. After the 1966 triumph, it was felt there was no need to change things after all, no need to get up to date, to copy methods or formations or ideas from anyone else. We were the champions.

Those players who won it for England that glorious day have grown better, bigger, more heroic, more honoured as the years have gone by – the main reason being that England has won so little since. Sometimes we've even failed to qualify, and often, when we did, we ended up playing rubbish. 1966 set us up, but it also set us back. It impeded progress and development for the next thirty years.

All English football fans now like to think that England is once more coming to the front as a world power, skilful, up to date, technically adept, fit and organised, capable of beating any nation on a good day, with the light and the right breeze behind us – even if with a foreign manager at the helm, something which could never have been imagined back in 1966.

I recently interviewed Sir Bobby Charlton, now aged sixty-five, for a BBC Radio 4 programme, and afterwards asked him what sort of money he was making, back in the Sixties. His best year was 1968, by which time he was a World Cup winner and a European Cup winner with Manchester United. In that year he earned roughly what a present-day England star makes in one day.

It's all ancient history now, what happened back in 1966, part of the dark ages when football and life were so different. Perhaps it's about time we started to forget it…

Overleaf: *England Captain Bobby Moore and his team celebrate winning the World Cup, Wembley, 1966*

Biographies

Simon Barnes

Simon Barnes is chief sportswriter for *The Times*. He has won a number of awards and currently holds the title of Sports Columnist of the Year. His third novel, *Miss Chance*, was recently re-issued in paperback. He lives in Suffolk with his family and rather a lot of horses.

Stephen Bayley

Stephen Bayley is a design consultant, author and ocean-going commentator. His Boilerhouse Project at the V&A was London's most popular gallery of the 1980s and the Design Museum that evolved from it a world first. His books include *In Good Shape*; *Sex, Drink and Fast Cars*; *Taste*; *Harley Earl*; and *Sex*. In 1989 he was made a Chevalier de l'Ordre des Arts et Lettres by the French Minister of Culture. He hates travelling quickly.

Dickie Bird

Dickie Bird has umpired 68 Test matches, set world records for umpiring 92 one-day internationals and 159 international matches, and is the only man to have umpired three World Cup cricket finals. Other major matches umpired include the Queen's Silver Jubilee Test Match (1977) and the Centenary Test Match (1980). A former player for Yorkshire and Leicestershire CCCs, he won Yorkshireman of the Year and People of the Year awards in 1996. He was awarded an MBE in 1986.

Mihir Bose

Mihir Bose is an author and journalist and senior columnist for the *Daily Telegraph*, specialising in sports business and political stories. He won the Sports Reporter of the Year Award in 1999 and is the author of some 20 books, including an award-winning *History of Indian Cricket*.

Ian Botham

Ian Botham is England's greatest all-round cricketer. During an international career that ran from 1977 to 1992 he played in 102 Tests, making 5,200 runs including 14 hundreds, and his 383 wickets, including 27 five-wicket innings, made him the most successful Test bowler in the history of English cricket. He reached the Test 'double' of 1,000 runs and 100 wickets in just 21 matches, a world record, and scored a century and took five wickets or more in a Test five times, another. He now works as a commentator for Sky Television.

Eddie Butler

Eddie Butler is rugby correspondent of the *Observer* and has contributed to BBC rugby reporting for many years.

Geoff Capes

Geoff Capes in the most capped British athlete of all time. He has held 17 titles, including British and Commonwealth Shot Put Champion and European Cup Champion; British, European and World Strongest Man; British, European and World Highland Games Champion; and Scottish Highland Games Champion. He was awarded the Queen's Jubilee Medal in 1977.

Bobby Charlton

England's highest ever goal-scorer, Bobby Charlton won 106 caps and scored 49 goals in his international footballing career. He scored 253 goals in 766 club appearances and was Manchester United's most capped player. A member of England's World Cup-winning team in 1966 and Manchester United's European Cup-winning team in 1968, he was also a League Championship winner in 1957, 1965 and 1967 and an FA Cup winner in 1963. He was knighted in 1994.

Henry Cooper

In a professional boxing career spanning 16 years, Henry Cooper won the British, European and Commonwealth heavyweight titles. He set a record by holding the British heavyweight title for 10 years 5 months, successfully defending it eight times, and was the first man ever to win three Lonsdale Belts. He also fought for the World Championship and was the first boxer to knock down the World Champion, Muhammad Ali. Henry Cooper was awarded the OBE in 1969 and was knighted in 2000.

Hunter Davies

Hunter Davies is the author of over 30 books, including *The Glory Game* – now considered one of the classic books about football – *A Walk around the Lakes*, and the only authorised biography of the Beatles. As a journalist, he currently writes a column about money in the *Sunday Times* and about football in the *New Statesman*.

Robert Edwards

Robert Edwards is the author of many books in the field of motor racing, including *Archie and the Listers*, which was voted book of the year and book of the decade by the motoring press. A regular contributor to *Motor Sport* and the *Daily Telegraph*, he is the author of *Stirling Moss: the Authorised Biography*.

Ginny Elliot

Ginny Elliot enjoyed a career as one of Britain's most successful equestrians. As Ginny Leng she won numerous competitions, including Badminton in 1985, 1989 and 1993, and Burghley in 1983, 1984 and 1986. She took first place and the Team Gold in the European Championships in 1985, 1987 and 1989, and in the World Championships in 1986, and the Team Silver in the Olympic Games in 1984 and 1988. She is the author of a number of books and was awarded an MBE in 1985.

Fergus Fleming

Fergus Fleming worked in publishing for six years before becoming a full-time writer in 1991. His books include *Barrow's Boys*, a history of British exploration in the nineteenth century, *Killing Dragons: the Conquest of the Alps*, and *Ninety Degrees North: the Quest for the North Pole*.

Tom Fort

Tom Fort worked in the BBC Radio Newsroom for 20 years and has been angling correspondent for the *Financial Times* for 14 years. He contributes to a wide range of sporting magazines, is editor of several fishing books, author of *The Far from Compleat Angler*, *The Grass Is Greener* (a social history of lawns and lawnmowing), and *The Book of the Eel*.

Dick Francis

Dick Francis is the author of more than 40 international bestsellers and is recognised as one of the world's finest thriller writers. His awards include the Crime Writers' Association's Cartier Diamond Dagger, and in 1996 he was made Mystery Writers of America Grand Master for a lifetime's achievement. He received a CBE in the 2000 Queen's Birthday Honours.

Brian Glanville

Brian Glanville is football writer for the *Sunday Times*, for whom he was football correspondent from 1958–92. For many years English correspondent of the *Corriere dello Sport* daily of Rome, he was also sports columnist at the *People* from 1992–6. He has covered the last 11 World Cups, and is the writer of *Story of the World Cup* and *Goal*, the official 1966 World Cup film. Among over 20 novels, *The Rise of Gerry Logan*, *The Dying of the Light*, *Target Man* and *Goalkeepers Are Different* have football subjects.

Duncan Goodhew

Duncan Goodhew began his international swimming career at the 1976 Montreal Olympic Games, where he finished sixth in the 100m breaststroke. He was the Great Britain and England swimming team captain from 1978–80 and won the Gold Medal in the 100m breaststroke in the 1980 Olympic Games in Moscow, where he also won Bronze in the 100m medley relay. He is the author of the book *Sink or Swim*, and was awarded an MBE for services to sport in 1981.

Andrew Graham-Dixon

The writer and broadcaster Andrew Graham-Dixon was chief art critic of the *Independent* from 1986–98 and is now chief art correspondent of the *Sunday Telegraph* magazine. His books include the bestselling *History of British Art* and *Renaissance*. During his misspent youth he spent much time at the Camden Snooker Centre, where he came to terms with the limited extent of his own talent for playing the game. His highest break is 96; it is a source of continuing irritation and sadness that he missed the red along the cushion which would, almost certainly, have given him his one and only century.

Jonathon Green

Jonathon Green is Britain's leading lexicographer of slang. Among his most recent books are the *Cassell Dictionary of Slang* (1998), the *Macmillan Dictionary of Contemporary Slang* (1996) and *Slang down the Ages: the Historical Development of Slang* (1993). His history of lexicography, *Chasing the Sun: Dictionary-makers and the Dictionaries They Made*, appeared in 1996. He is also co-author with Don Atyeo of the *Book of Sports Quotes*. His current project is the multi-volumed *Cassell Historical Dictionary of Slang*.

Reg Gutteridge

Reg Gutteridge comes from a boxing family and won several amateur titles. He became boxing correspondent of the *Evening News* in 1951 and a commentator in the early 1960s, appearing on the first *World of Sport* in 1965. He covered six Olympic Games and probably more Muhammad Ali fights than any other commentator. He was awarded an OBE in 1995 for services to boxing broadcasting and journalism and was inducted into the International Boxing Hall of Fame in the USA in 2002.

Duff Hart-Davis

Duff Hart-Davis is a countryman with a lifelong interest in shooting and conservation. He contributed the weekly 'Country Matters' column to the *Independent* from 1986–2001 and is the author of over 30 books, including *Monarchs of the Glen*, a history of deer-stalking in the Scottish Highlands. He has also written biographies of the author and traveller Peter Fleming, the sporting artist Raoul Millais, and Eileen Soper, who painted badgers, deer, birds and other wildlife in watercolours.

Peter Hayter

Peter Hayter is cricket correspondent of the *Mail on Sunday*, having previously written for the *Observer* and the *Independent* and for *Sportsweek Magazine* as their football correspondent. He is the author of a number of books on cricket, having collaborated with Ian Botham on his bestselling autobiography *Don't Tell Kath* and two other books *The Botham Report* and *Botham's Century* and with Phil Tufnell on his autobiography *What Now?* and *Postcards from the Beach*. His other books include *England's Cricket Heroes* and *Great Tests Recalled*.

Rupert Isaacson

Rupert Isaacson raised enough money to buy his first horse by running a junk stall in a flea market at the age of 12. Since then he has hunted, evented, show-jumped and studied dressage all over the world. He has been an environment and human rights journalist in Africa, notably with the Bushmen of the Kalahari, and works with shamanic healers there and in other parts of the world. He is the author of *The Healing Land* and *The Wild Host: the History and Meaning of the Hunt*.

Ken Jones

A former professional footballer, Ken Jones has been covering sport for more than 40 years. He joined the *Daily Mirror* as a football writer in 1958, later moving to the *Sunday Mirror* as chief sports writer/ columnist. He took up a similar

post with the *Independent* on its launch in 1986. Since retiring in 1998 he has continued to serve the paper as a freelance columnist.

Frank Keating

Frank Keating has been sports columnist for the *Guardian* since 1970, after spending time as an independent television producer. He has been named Sports Writer of the Year on several occasions.

Christopher Martin-Jenkins

Christopher Martin-Jenkins has been chief cricket correspondent for *The Times* since 1999 and BBC cricket commentator since 1973. He is the author of many books on cricket, including *The Wisden Book of Cricket* (1981); *Cricket: a Way of Life* (1984); *Cricket Characters* (1987); and, jointly, *Summers Will Never Be the Same* (1994), a tribute to Brian Johnston.

Lord Montagu of Beaulieu

The son of a leading British motoring pioneer, Lord Montagu founded the Montagu Motor Museum in memory of his father. It became the National Motor Museum in 1972. Lord Montagu is president of the Federation of British Historic Vehicle Clubs and the Historic Commercial Vehicle Society, honorary vice-president of the Veteran Car Club of Great Britain and a member of the Guild of Motoring Writers. His many books include *The Horseless Carriage*; *Early Days on the Road*; *Home, James*; and *The British Motorist*.

Stephen Moss

Stephen Moss was born in Newport, Monmouthshire, in 1957. He studied modern history at Balliol College, Oxford, and has an MA in Victorian Studies from Birkbeck College, London. He is

on the staff of the *Guardian*, of which he was literary editor, and is currently writing a cultural history of sport. He plays cricket for the *Observer* (est. 1791) and for Ham and Petersham CC (est. 1815). He has also hunted with the Beaufort, tilted on Icelandic ponies and played polo in Virginia, narrowly surviving on each occasion.

Sue Mott

Sue Mott has been sportswriter for the *Daily Telegraph* since 1994. Formerly with the *Sunday Times*, the *Australian*, the *New York Daily News*, the *San Francisco Chronicle* and the *Seattle Times*, she was voted Sports Feature Writer of the Year in 1995. She co-presented BBC2's sports investigative programme *On the Line*, and is the author of *Girl's Guide to Ball Games*.

Peter Nichols

Peter Nichols spent ten years at sea working as a professional yacht captain, living and cruising aboard his own small wooden sailboat, before turning to writing full time. He is the author of three critically acclaimed books: a memoir of those years, *Sea Change: Alone across the Atlantic in a Wooden Boat*; a novel, *Lodestar*; and the bestseller, *A Voyage for Madmen*, about the 1968–9 *Sunday Times* Golden Globe Race.

Richard Noble

As the founder and only director of SSC Programme Ltd, Richard Noble achieved the first ever supersonic world land speed record in 1997 with the ThrustSSC team and the 110,000hp ThrustSSC car driven by Andy Green. He was also the chairman and managing director of Thrust Cars Ltd, driving Thrust2 at over 600 mph 11 times to a peak speed of 650 mph. A specialist in motivational and leadership presentations involving teamwork, he is the author of *Fastest Man on Earth* (1984) and *THRUST* (1998).

Robin Oakley

Formerly the political editor of *The Times* and of the BBC and now European political editor of CNN, Robin Oakley is a long-time racing enthusiast. For seven years he has written a weekly racing column for the *Spectator* and he is also a columnist for the *Racing Review*. He is the author of *Valley of the Racehorse* (2000), a portrait of the racing community in Lambourn, and has been a part-owner of some not very good racehorses.

Terry O'Connor

Terry O'Connor worked for the London *Evening News* and the *Daily Mail* for 36 years, during which time he covered 11 Olympic Games, mainly as chief athletics writer. His distinguished rugby writing includes coverage of 11 British Lions tours.

Simon Rae

Simon Rae is a poet, playwright, biographer and broadcaster. His *W. G. Grace: A Life* (1998) was acclaimed as the definitive biography of 'The Champion' and shared the Cricket Society's Literary Award. *It's Not Cricket: Skulduggery, Sharp Practice and Downright Cheating in the Noble Game* (2001) was shortlisted for the same award. He won the National Poetry Prize in 1999, and is the author of two plays, *A Quiet Night In* and *Grass*.

Angela Rippon

Angela Rippon is one of the best known faces and voices in British broadcasting. Appointed the first woman journalist newsreader by the BBC in 1975, she was a founder member of the commercial breakfast television service TV-am in 1982 and worked in America before joining LBC Radio in 1990. She currently works for BBC TV's Watchdog unit on *Healthcheck* and hosts a new family finance channel, *Simply Money*. She is chairman of English National Ballet.

Graham Spiers

Graham Spiers is a writer and broadcaster, based in Glasgow, where he is chief sports writer for the *Herald*. He was formerly chief sportswriter with *Scotland on Sunday*, and is four-times winner of the Sports Writer of the Year title in the Scottish Press Awards.

Daniel Topolski

Daniel Topolski is a writer and broadcaster on travel and sport. He has written five books – about Africa, South America, the Boat Race, the Oxford Boat Race mutiny and Henley. He rowed in the Boat Race in 1967 and 1968 and six times for Great Britain, winning Gold and Silver in 1977 and 1975. He coached Oxford to 12 victories in the Boat Race between 1974 and 1987, and coached the British men's and women's crews four times at the Olympics and World Championships.

Virginia Wade

Virginia Wade was the number one-ranked tennis player in Great Britain for ten consecutive years and won the Ladies Singles Championship at Wimbledon in 1977. She achieved a total of seven Grand Slam titles, including the Singles at the US Open in 1968, and went on to win the Australian Championship in 1972. In 1989 she was inducted into the International Tennis Hall of Fame. She has been a regular commentator at major tennis championships for a variety of television companies, including the BBC.

Alan Watkins

Alan Watkins was born in 1933 and educated at Amman Valley Grammar School and Queens' College, Cambridge. He has been a journalist since 1959 and has written a weekly political column since 1963, most recently in the *Independent on Sunday*. He also writes a rugby column in the *Independent*. He is the author of seven books, of which the latest is *A Short Walk down Fleet Street*.

Colin Welland

Colin Welland is a highly successful actor, playwright and writer for both television and films. Among his most memorable plays are *Bangelstein's Boys, Roll on Four O'Clock, Say Goodnight to Grandma* and *Leeds United*, and his films include *A Dry White Season* and the Academy Award-winning *Chariots of Fire*.

J P R Williams

J P R Williams played for Bridgend Rugby Football Club from 1967–8 and 1976–81, and for London Welsh RFC from 1968–76. With Barbarians Wales from 1969–81, he won 55 caps and was a member of the British Lions tours in New Zealand in 1971 and South Africa in 1974. He played in all eight Tests. He was also British Junior Champion at Wimbledon in 1966. J P R Williams retired from rugby in 1981 and has been consultant orthopaedic surgeon at Bridgend Sports Clinic since 1986.

Acknowledgments

First published in 2002 by
Cassell Illustrated
Octopus Publishing Group Limited
2–4 Heron Quays, London E14 4JP

A CIP catalogue record for this book is available from the British Library.
ISBN 1 844 03041 5

Commissioning Editor:
Annabel Merullo has spent her career working in television and book publishing. She is the co-creator of the successful series of Century books, including *The Russian Century*, *The British Century* and *The Chinese Century*. She was also the commissioning editor of *British Greats*.

Consultant Editor:
Neil Wenborn is a full-time writer and publishing consultant. Co-editor of the *Companion to British History*, he has published biographies of Mozart, Haydn and Stravinsky and was the consultant editor of *British Greats*.

Assistant Editor: Victoria Alers-Hankey
Designer: Nigel Soper

Printed and bound in Italy

The publisher would like to thank the following for permission to reproduce their material. Every care has been taken to trace copyright holders. However, if we have omitted anyone we apologise and shall, if informed, make corrections in any future edition.

Page 9 Kobal Collection; 13 The Alpine Club; 16–17 Kobal Collection; 19 Allsport/Getty Images; 22 Allsport/Getty Images; 24 Empics/Alpha; 29 Allsport/Getty Images; 33 Allsport/Getty Images; 37 Getty Images; 39 Allsport/Getty Images; 43 Chichester Archives/PPL; 44 Bridgeman Art Library; 48–49 Getty Images; 52-3 Popperfoto; 55 Topham Picture Library; 58-9 Bridgeman Art Library/Phillips Auctioneers; 63 BBC Picture Archives; 67 Empics/Alpha; 69 Getty Images; 74–5 Getty Images; 76 Bridgeman Art Library/ Marylebone Cricket Club; 81 Allsport/Getty Images; 84 Getty Images; 87 Advertising Archives; 91 Getty Images; 94–95 Bridgeman Art Library/ Christies; 98 BBC Picture Archives; 99 Empics; 101 Bridgeman Art Library/Lambeth Palace Library; 105 Getty Images; 108–9 Kobal Collection; 112-3 Bridgeman Art Library/Marylebone Cricket Club; 116 Allsport/Getty Images; 121 Getty Images; 123 Empics; 126–127 Allsport/Getty Images; 130–131 Getty Images; 134 Getty Images; 139 Getty Images; 142–143 Allsport/Getty Images; 145 Getty Images; 148 Allsport/Getty Images; 152–153 Getty Images; 156 Allsport/Getty Images; 159 Empics; 163 Stirling Moss Collection; 165 Getty Images; 170–171 Allsport/Getty Images; 174 Allsport/Getty Images; 177 Allsport/Getty Images; 180 Bridgeman Art Library/Marylebone Cricket Club; 186–187 Empics.